BRAISHFIELD MEMORIES

2003

BRAISHFIELD MEMORIES

was compiled and edited by

Susan Buxton

Hannah Boothman   Jill Fahy
Ann Chant   Tessa Allen   Rosie Groves

Line drawings by **Alan Olden**

Published by Braishfield Memories

ISBN 0-9546295-0-7

This collection copyright © Braishfield Parish Council 2003

Every effort has been made to contact copyright holders of material reproduced in this book. We apologise to any that we have not been able to trace.

All rights reserved. No part of this publication may be reproduced, stored in or introduced into a retrieval system, or transmitted, in any form, or by any means (electronic, mechanical, photocopying, recording or otherwise) without the prior written permission of the publisher. Any person who does any unauthorized act in relation to this publication may be liable to criminal prosecution and civil claims for damages.

A CIP catalogue record for this book is available from the British Library.

Designed by Helen Moss
Printed and bound in Great Britain by BAS Printers Ltd, Salisbury, Wiltshire

Contents

Introduction		vii
History		viii
Acknowledgements		x
Map		xi
Anon	From the Top of Crook Hill	1
Betsy Ashton	The Austerity Years	6
Dorothy Bacon	Braishfield in the 1920s	9
	Vanished Buildings	13
Geoff Baird	The Braishfield Hoopmakers	16
Joan Bartlam	Our Lovely Village	20
Anne Beggs	The Evacuee	23
Barbara Bell	Twinning with Crouay	26
Samuel Boothman	A Rector's Perspective	29
Ann Chant	The Braishfield School Log Books	35
	School	44
Tony Chant	The Square in Norman Thelwell's Time	47
Janet Cook	Farmers and Farming	51
	Farming	57
Alma Fail	The Carpenter's Daughter	61
Pat Foxcroft	The Blacksmith's Daughter	65
Norman Goodland	From a Countryman's Diary	72
Dilys Grieve	Elm Grove Childhood	78
	People	83
Clara Alice Hayter	A Schoolgirl in the Twenties	87
Fannie Holbrook	A Lifetime in One Place	91
Roy Hughes	The Braishfield Country Fair	96
Eric Irish	Fire at the Dog and Crook	104
Cherry McCall	A Glimpse of the 1970s	109
	Organisations	110

Kate Marshall	Filming 'Worzel Gummidge'	115
Robin Merton	The War Years	120
Ena Ninnim &		
Maggie Batchelor	The Glister Sisters	125
Malcolm Norman	Guns and Wheels	136
Dave Old	The Football Club	138
	Teams	144
Joan Parsons	The Landgirl	148
Wendy Quarendon	Two Village Shops	151
Sally Rawson-Smith	The Hunt	153
Jane Rogers	The Fernhill Roman Bath-House Dig	157
John Saunders	The Builder	160
	Buildings	175
Sidney Scorey	The Verger	179
Tony Stares	The Bowns of Braishfield	192
Doug Stewart	2:30 at the War Memorial	195
Margaret Stewart	The Braishfield Seven	197
	Events	199
Rita Stitt & Margaret Old	Rita and Girlie	204
June Thomson	The Braishfield House Fire	215

Introduction

Whether we come over the brow of Crook Hill, wind down the lane from Slackstead past Woolley Green, approach from Casbrook towards Lower Street and Newport Lane, or descend the long hill from Kings Somborne, as the view opens out, our special corner of the Hampshire countryside appears, and we know we have arrived back home.

Braishfield is home to a community of some five hundred people. Families and buildings have come and gone, economic and social influences have wrought great changes, none greater than during the twentieth century, but the village community has endured.

Ours is at least the second and possibly the third attempt to gather memories and impressions of our village. We are indebted to those who started collecting memories more than thirty years ago and to the Braishfield Women's Institute who kept the material safe and passed it to us. We are also grateful to the Braishfield Village Association News whose editor has given permission to reprint some of the contributions.

Memory is fallible and elusive. We all remember events slightly differently and we tend to be selective. What is published here is not history but individual recollections containing vivid impressions of events and personalities, and reminders of a life which as altered considerably. We are conscious that many aspects of village life have not been mentioned; the book has been shaped by the memories and photographs given to us.

Those who are reading about Braishfield for the first time will learn of a village whose way of life has changed markedly in the last century and the memory of whose characters, occupations and rural existence is rapidly disappearing. For those who know the village we hope this book will bring back happy memories of your own. We are always interested in collecting additional information which can be added to the village archive.

We present this collection of memories at the beginning of a new millennium as a tribute to Braishfield past and present, remembering those who have gone before us and whose endeavours have made the village we know today.

History

Although the ecclesiastical parish of Braishfield was only formed in 1855 and the civil parish just under a century later there is evidence of human activity in the area in the Paleolithic era, about 500,000 years ago. At Broom Hill there is evidence of intermittent settlement from the late Paleolithic, Mesolithic, Neolithic, Bronze Age, Iron Age, Roman and late Saxon periods. The site is particularly noted for the range and quality of Mesolithic flint tools, and it would have been visited seasonally by Mesolithic hunter-gatherers. In later periods of settled agricultural activity, from the Neolithic period onwards, the site would have been inhabited for longer periods.

The Romans settled at Fernhill not far from the Mesolithic site. A late third century bath house was excavated in 1976, part of a much older villa complex consisting of at least six substantial buildings which were occupied long before the construction of the bath house.

Little is recorded of Braishfield until 1043 when, as part of the manor of Michelmersh, the lands were donated by Queen Emma to the cathedral clergy at Winchester. Later much of this holding was released to secular landowners, including two Oxford colleges, one of which owned land in the village up to the Second World War.

The origin of the name Braishfield is not clear. The name Braisflede, meaning 'brow of hill' or 'open land or fields', is first documented in 1235, but some believe that the name is derived from 'brassy fields' where 'brassy' means soil of poor quality or flinty. Indeed many Braishfield-born people still call it 'Brashfield'.

In the Middle Ages Braishfield consisted of a number of large but scattered farmsteads, some of which survive today, including Pitt Farm, Elm Grove, Sharpes Farm, Fairbournes Farm, Paynes Hay and Hall Place. Fairbournes Farm is believed to be the oldest of these, dating from the tenth century. Archeological evidence suggests that Hall Place was a major fourteenth century manor site. There were two large commons in the village before the Enclosures in 1794, Casbrook to the west and Braishfield Common, a one hundred and thirty-eight acre area covering most of the southern part of the present village from the site of the War Memorial. The oldest buildings with medieval origins are to be found around the periphery of these ancient commons.

The Parish Church of All Saints' was built in the gothic style in 1855 designed by a prominent Victorian architect, William Butterfield. At that time there were already three non-conformist chapels in the village only one of which remains as the United Reformed Church, built in 1818. The Braishfield Public Elementary School was opened in 1877 bringing public education to the village children, although there were two small schools in the village prior to this date.

Twentieth century Braishfield experienced gradual development as the areas between the old cottages and farmsteads were filled with new houses. Since the Second World War the pace of change increased and, in common with much of rural Britain, there was a transition from a predominantly agricultural community with the majority of inhabitants living and working within the village to one which is primarily a residential area with most people travelling away to work.

Acknowledgements

This book has been produced by the Braishfield Memories Committee, a hard-working group of six. The driving force behind the committee has always been Susan Buxton whose enthusiasm and persistence has meant that memories accumulated over many years have finally been brought to publication. This book owes its existence to her.

The core of the book is the wonderful collection of memories. We appreciate the time, care and effort which have gone into recording the vivid recollections spanning the last century, each with its own voice.

We are grateful to all those who have given access to their family photographs and who have generously allowed us to use them in the book. Many people have gone out of their way to search for elusive photographs for us. Our thanks also to those who took part in the major exercise of scanning and printing copies of the photographs collected; during the compiling of the book we have collected over six hundred photographs. An archive of those of village importance will be created with the help of Greg Smith and given to the Hampshire Record Office.

We have relied on the local knowledge of many people to enable us to create captions to enhance the photographs and complement the memories. Every time we phoned or appeared on the doorstep to ask yet another question we were met with unfailing courtesy and helpfulness.

Finally, we would like to pay tribute to Jon Stone for his encouragement, flair and creativity so freely given at the initial design stages of the book.

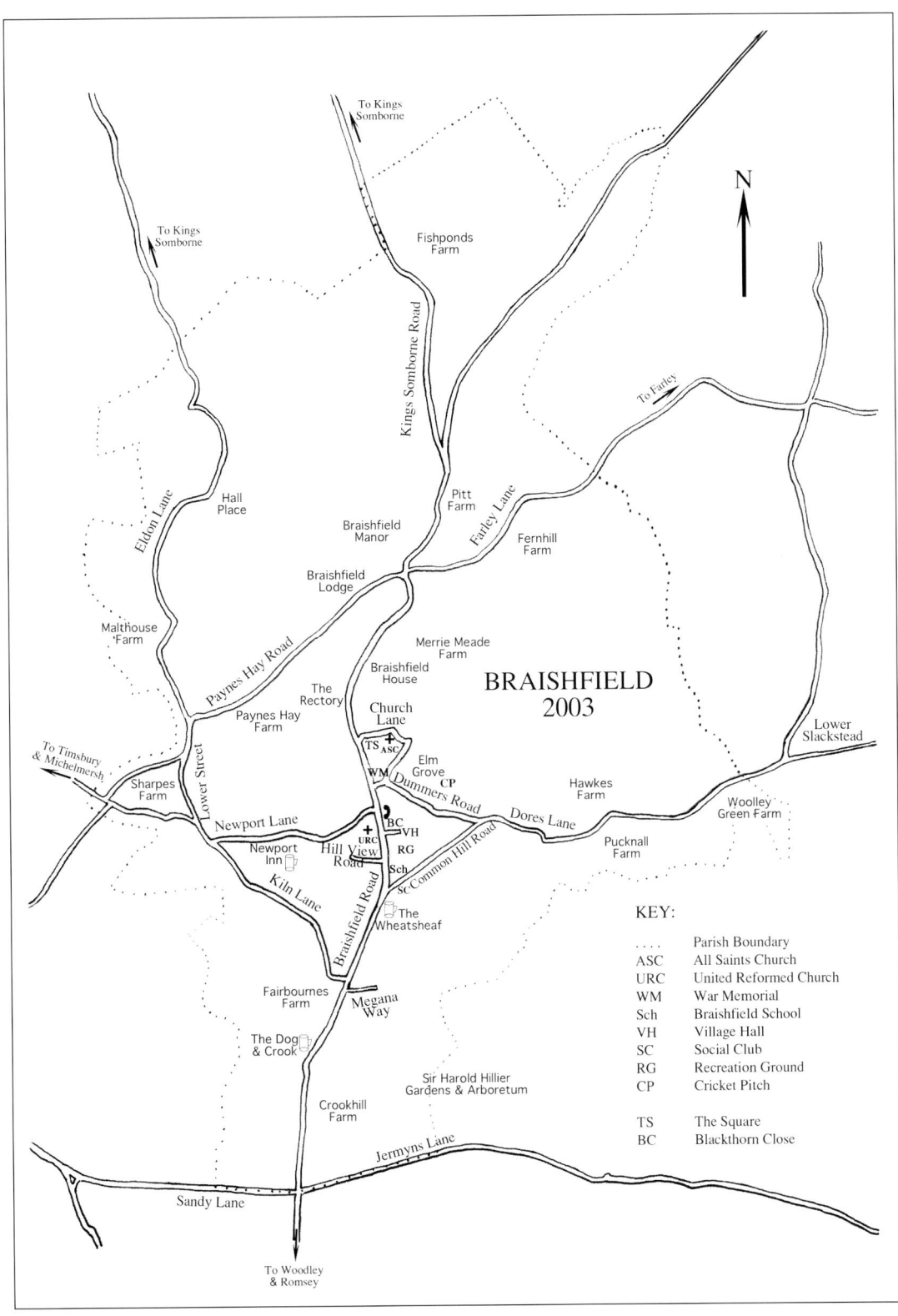

From the Top of Crook Hill
Anon

1850–1940

On the west side of Crook Hill there was a brick kiln owned by Mr Prince of Romsey. It was in full use until about 1902. Further up the road, just over the bridge on the right, is the residence where Mr Grace lived who carried on the job of well-boring. That business closed down about 1930. This Mr Grace paid to have the Chapel enlarged in 1906.

Now we are at the Wheatsheaf. The landlord, on 5th November, had a bonfire in the field in front of the house. After this big heap of bushes had burnt there was a patch of red-hot ashes about twenty feet wide. Then two lads ran across over the cinders. One of them was tripped by a partly burnt stick and fell down on the red-hot cinders burning both hands and scorching his face. He was rushed to the doctor for treatment. This was the last bonfire here. This lad's name was Harry Hooper and he lived at Pucknall with his parents in the residence now named Bramble Cottage.

Now to Dummers House in the 1890s. This is where Mr Charles Cooper lived and carried on business as a wood and coal dealer. They had a family of five boys. One took over the pub and farm at Newport Lane and another was teacher for several years at Braishfield School. This plot of ground is now used for the Hursley Foxhound Kennels.

A postcard sent in 1907 of Crook Bridge looking north.

Braishfield Road looking north in the early 1900s. The house on the left was called South View, then Tiffany Cottage, now Swallowfield, after the fields beside it. The extension on the road was a shop and post office and there was a bakery behind. Number 1 Newport Lane can be seen in the middle distance. The photo is marked 'Brashfield' which is the local pronunciation of Braishfield.

Back in the 1890s there was a thatched cottage for two families standing on high ground at Fern Hill which was about two hundred years old. In the early 1900s one tenant built a wooden structure bungalow for himself and wife on a plot of ground nearby as the old house was getting shaky. About twelve years later it was burnt down. The wife had the copper alight and the wooden wall near the copper caught alight. Then their home was soon a heap of ashes. They built another on the same ground.

Farther on is Pucknall Farm. This is where the village cricket team played on the lawn back in the 1880s.

Now to Woolley House on the hill. Back in the mid-1800s this building was a college. In later years it caught fire and burnt the school end of the building. That finished the college. The remaining building was made into a private residence.

Then farther on, turning left to Slackstead, the house on the corner back in the 1890s was where the carter lived that worked at the nearby farm. In the 1880s or earlier at a spot just inside the copse on the sharp bend of the road was where Ned, the hurdler and sparmaker worked. It was at that time nearly all sheep farms. The farmers brought their rods here for Ned to make hurdles and spars for them, so this spot was named Ned's Corner. He lived in the Woodman's Cottage at Farley where, in later years, Walter Brown lived.

Now back to the main road. The oak tree in the school playground was planted in 1904 by Mr Owen of Elm Grove Farm, John and Bill Harris of Hall Farm and Moses Sargent of the Wheatsheaf Inn with, of course, a jar of beer. This tree, standing about five feet high, was brought from Bull Grove Copse. Next is the shop near the chapel. It was the baker and grocer's business of Mr W Fielder.

Cottages on the north side of The Square in the early 1900s. Church Lane drops down on the left of the building. The bargeboard of Orchard Lodge can be seen in the background. These cottages were joined into one residence in the 1960s and named Orchard Rise. Forge Cottage is on the right.

The building in Newport Lane that is now used as an engineers' shop was a chapel back in the 1890s. Mr Scorey, who lived in the 1890s with his wife and four children at Number 1 Newport Lane, was sexton and gravedigger at Braishfield Church and he was then drummer in the village band. The post office was at Number 2, you can see from the road where the letter box was by a mark on the wall to the left of the door.

Then farther along the main road on the corner was the coal business of Mr George Saunders that was finished with several years ago. The War Memorial stands at the corner on ground that was part of the garden.

Farther on again is the shop that was carried on some years ago by Mr Caleb Abraham, his son and daughter as a baker's, grocer's and off-licence. This is The Square, the centre of the village. There was a blacksmith's shop on the right. It's now a bungalow. On the left was the boot and shoe repair shop. Both shops were finished with in the mid-1940s. Then there was Turp Brown, the timber carter, who lived at the residence now named Orchard Rise. The stable was round at the back of his house under the same roof. The horses had to pass by close to the back door to get to the stable. Some seventy years ago the chimney of the house was struck by lightning. When it was repaired an iron clamp was fixed near the top of the chimney as a lightning conductor.

In the 1890s the Lessons at the church were read by Mr Frank Bailey of Colsons Farm. The clock in the church tower was bought by public

Orchard Cottage between the wars viewed from the top of Church Lane.

Chalk Pit Cottages in 1953, taken from the south, is so known because of the large chalk pit across the road to the east which in 2002 was filled in. Chalk pits, some of which are very old, are features of the village which is situated on the edge of the chalk downland.

* forshore – It has not been possible to trace a definition of this word. Its likely meaning is a bit of waste wood from a piece used as a shore or prop.

subscription. Mr Frank Bailey was the leading official and it was fixed there in the late 1890s. Years later the farm was taken over by Mr and Mrs Lush. They had an army torch light display in the meadow in front of their house which they had named The Cottage. It is now pulled down.

Now to Orchard Cottage. About seventy-five years ago a man and wife lived here by the name of Gear. He was a farm labourer. When he was round the fields if he saw a loose stick poked in the hedge he would pull it out and take it home for the fire. A young gent just for a game put a small charge of gunpowder in the end of an old forshore* and put it in the hedge so it could be seen. Gear saw it and took it home for the fire. The wife put it in and the kettle was soon blown off. No damage was done but the young gent had a lecture from his father.

On to Chalkpit Cottage. About half-way between the cottage and the road there was a sawpit, a big hole in the ground with timber across, and a big barn that was used for storing the cut timber. The barn was pulled down and the pit filled in back in the 1890s.

Pitt House, which is now named the Manor, was where Mr Newton lived. He had a windmill built by Mr Grace, mentioned earlier, in a field by the side of Dark Lane, to supply water to Pitt House and the Lodge.

Miss Hill lived at Braishfield Lodge back in the 1880s. She was a good friend to the old people of the village and a regular follower with the Hursley Foxhounds. In the field near the Lodge she had her ponies buried and a fir tree still stands there. She was buried in Braishfield churchyard in 1898. It was said she chose the spot where she should be laid to rest.

Pitt House viewed from the crossroads before the wings were added in 1910 by Mr and Mrs King. Since the early part of the twentieth century it has been called Braishfield Manor. The iron railings surrounding the park are said to have been melted down for the 1914/18 war effort. Dark Lane leads up the hill from the crossroads on the right past Windmill Cottages on the brow of the hill.

In 1912 there was a fire in the cornfield on the Lodge side of Bowling Green Road. The field was rented by Bentley George of Hall Farm. The carter was there with two horses and binder cutting the corn. They were getting near the end when the manager of the farm and a friend walked in from the road. A fire started from the track the men were coming up and burnt the patch of standing corn. The carter was able to get the horses and binder to safety. He made for the hedge and all was well.

This memory is believed to have been written by Henry William (Ibby) Dewey (1888–1976) in the 1970s and was held in safekeeping by the WI. Mr Dewey and his wife lived at 3 Common Hill.

The Congregational Church, erected in 1818. It is often referred to as 'the chapel' in the village. An extension was added in 1906 instigated by Mr James Grace, an artesian well-borer and benefactor of the Congregational Church. It is possibly for this reason that the words inscribed over the door of the new extension are, "Whosoever will, let him take the water of life freely". Rev.22.17. In the year 2000 the chapel was connected at last to the mains water supply when a cloakroom was added, known as 'Vera's Room', in memory of Vera Rampley, the organist for many years.

The Austerity Years
Betsy Ashton

1944–1951

Mrs Ashton and her daughter, Betsy, in the late 1940s taken at a wedding.

Coming to live in the village was the first time I had moved house, so it was all strange and exciting. I was twelve years old when we came to Braishfield Manor.

Petrol was rationed, and if we wanted to go to the station we used to book Mr Jet Goulding. His sister used to take the bookings; she never wrote anything down that I remember and he never missed out. He would drive at speed along the lanes and try to run over any rabbits that crossed in front of him, especially alongside the field of black sheep kept by Sir George Cooper on our way to Winchester up through Farley, down to Berry Down and along the valley. Mr Goulding and his sister lived at Pucknall House where the Whites are. He lived at the road end and she lived

Dummers, now Pucknall House, in 1904 when it was a Hursley Estate cottage, 182 Pucknall. The Hursley Estate once extended well into Braishfield as far as the present Social Club in Common Hill. Many of the houses on the estate were built with characteristic features such as the decorative brick chimneys and lozenge-shaped window panes. Pucknall House is a typical example. The Goulding family, who lived there for over fifty years, are pictured outside. Left to right: Mary Goulding, Eva Williams, aged two (later Eva Fielder), Fanny Williams (born Goulding) and Jesse (Jet) Goulding.

A group of Women's Institute members and their families taken outside the WI Hall in the early 1950s. The hall was demolished in the 1980s and houses built on the site, which is just south of The Square. Left to right: Back row: Mrs White (in hat), Mrs George Dummer, Mrs Frank Dunning, Evelyn Cook, Mrs Cook (in hat), Doreen Fielder holding Michael, Mrs Dunford, ?, Joyce Alford, ?, ? partly hidden, ?, ? partly hidden, Beryl Dunning, Madge Old, ? with hat. Middle row: Seated: Mrs Benham senior, Maisie Benham, ?, ?, ?, ?, ?, ?. Front row: children: Elizabeth Benham, Jean Benham, ?, Jim Windibank, John Fielder (baby on lap), ?, Mary Windibank (little girl in white dress).

at the other end. She took in laundry, which was always hanging out on a line going down toward the stream. Her daughter, Mrs Fielder, lived in Hursley where her husband worked for the Hursley Estate.

My grandfather lived in Cambridge and had to get a permit to come and visit as we were in a different zone, being close to Southampton, though the people who lived in Southampton were referred to as foreigners by the villagers!

Our house shared a water supply with the farm and Braishfield Lodge next door. In dry spells the well got very low and the cows took priority until the rain set things to rights again. I can remember a conversation when Lady Bacon came to ask whether it was all right to start baths again, or if the farm still needed all the water.

One job, which came round regularly, was going along to the baker to see if the bread had come. Delivery was supposed to be in the morning, but was very erratic, and could be much later on. We usually bicycled and as there was not much traffic we had the lanes to ourselves. We took our roller skates onto the road once, thinking it was a better surface than the gravel by the house, and got well scolded by Dr Johnson who found us as he turned the corner in his car!

My mother helped with the Infant Welfare Clinic at the WI Hut, and I would go too, to weigh babies or just hold them while people were busy. It was a good centre of information, and held the community together, though at the time I just thought it was nice to play with the little ones. She also went to help at local hospitals in Michelmersh where the army had taken over the big house.

There was said to be a grey or white lady who walked at night along the lower lane near our orchard. We never saw her, and didn't try very hard, but she was supposed to be someone who had lived in our house long ago and not been happy. I am sure someone knew much more than we learned.

Several ghost stories exist around this area. Another version related to Norman Thelwell by the gardener at Braishfield Lodge tells of a lady in a green crinoline dress who lost her fiancé.

Betsy and her two brothers, Jeremy and Simon, moved to the Manor in 1944 with their widowed mother, Isabel Ashton. Mrs Ashton, who was much involved in the life of the village and served as a church-warden, died in 1951 and the Manor was sold. Betsy pursued a career in nursing and now lives in a village near Farnham.

Her elder brother, Jeremy, took holy orders and after serving as a missionary in Papua New Guinea he was appointed Bishop of Aipo Rongo in 1977. He visited All Saints' Church the following summer with his wife and family, bringing with him his bishop's cope made of tree bark!

Braishfield in the 1920s
Dorothy Bacon (1906–1998)

1919–1930

It was the spring of 1919 when my mother and I found ourselves on the platform of Romsey Station wondering what on earth we were going to do next. It had been planned to spend the Easter holidays with friends as, although my parents had bought the Lodge, barring two beds and some few bits and pieces brought by the Alfords who were in residence, the house was completely devoid of furniture. To add to our joy I had produced whooping cough therefore, naturally, we could not inflict ourselves on anyone and so hopefully we came home. What next!

Luckily, and by the merest chance, Mrs King who lived at the Manor was at the station and after insisting that we spent the first night with her she lent us everything from teaspoons to blankets, and so we lived for three weeks until our own furniture started to arrive.

Braishfield at that time was a quiet, agricultural little village with a population of about two hundred and eighty. Naturally there were none of the amenities with which we are so accustomed these days. No piped waters – everyone had their own well – and we at the Lodge were served by the one at Windmill Cottage

Miss Dorothy Bacon in ATS uniform in 1944.

which fed the Manor, ourselves, Paynes Hay Farm and Mrs King's stud of hackney ponies. This was splendid until, as frequently happened during the hot weather, the pump broke down. Panic stations! Then gradually, to the relief of all, water was brought to the village with stand pipes from which the inhabitants could draw what they wanted.

Oil lamps and candles were the order of the day, and even after electricity was brought to the village one old lady refused to have anything to do with it and insisted on keeping her old lamps although she was very old and practically blind. This, as can well be understood, caused great consternation in the village lest she should have an accident and burn herself badly.

The great excitement was when we tried to get the telephone installed. My father applied in the usual way, and after the normal delay he was told that if he could get five subscribers they would consider the matter. Well, believe it or not, only three people were prepared to take the risk, so that was that for the time being. Later he tried again only to be told this time that if he could find seven potential subscribers they might consider the matter!! The natural reaction of the Admiral to this was, "If I can't find five how the blue-pencil do you imagine I can find seven?" Anyhow persistence and perseverance prevailed and a call-box was eventually installed with Mr King and my father guaranteeing fifty pounds, and at the end of the first year they had to pay up twenty-five pounds!! Naturally, as always happens, once the villagers appreciated what a real convenience it was subscribers flowed in and the exchange now covers three or four villages.

The WI started in 1921 and my mother was the first president, a position she held for twenty years. Last year we enjoyed our Golden Jubilee.

Whilst still at school I got permission from the then District Commissioner of the Girl Guides, Lady Melchett, to form a holiday patrol and Lily Old (now Martin) and Alice Miles (now Travis) became my first guides. As soon as I left school this developed into a proper company – The First Braishfield and Farley. However, as I went abroad each year, sadly it became impossible for it to carry on.

The headmaster of the school was Mr Carpenter whose wife also played the organ in Braishfield Church.

Lady Cooper of Hursley Park opening the Braishfield Horticultural Society Flower Show in 1938. The show was held in a field opposite the school. Lady Cooper, WG Owen and AC Dane are in the foreground. Among others in the background are Mr Young, E Webb, Percival Old and A Lawes.

Admiral Sir Reginald and Lady Bacon and Miss Dorothy Bacon at Braishfield Lodge in the early 1940s.

We had a very flourishing flower show held annually in a field which is now Hill View. Our excellent secretary, Mr Dane, carried on until the Second World War after which, as it was impossible to find another secretary, the flower show sadly lapsed.

One of the village shops was owned by Mr Thorne and the other by Miss Abraham whose brother Freddie also ran the bakery at the rear of these premises. There was a further bakery at Lower Street operated by Mr Harry Fielder.

Mr Fred Fielder was in charge of the post office situated in the house opposite Braishfield Garage*, and as it was reckoned to be exactly one

* **Braishfield Garage was demolished in 2002 and replaced by the new houses in Blackthorn Close.**

The dedication of the Braishfield War Memorial in 1921. Known faces: Admiral Bacon (saluting), The Reverend E R Chamney (Vicar of Braishfield), The Reverend J G Tuckey (Assistant Chaplain General to the Forces), The Reverend D Lewys Thomas (Romsey Congregational Minister) and T H Lush and E J Lovelace (churchwardens). Mr Lush donated the site for the War Memorial. "Wreaths were laid on the steps of the memorial until they were completely covered. In the front was a laurel wreath from the children and staff of the school."
Extract from the Romsey Advertiser, 18th March 1921.

The cast of the WI Drama Group's production of 'The Wife of Bath's Tale' on the stage in the WI Hall in the mid-1970s. Miss Bacon, who was a keen amateur player, is pictured in the title role, second from left, middle row. Left to right: Back row: Fiona Freckleton, Nick Shepherd, Jean Fielder, Moira Connolly, John Poolford, Pat Rowe. Middle row: Mary Boothman, Dorothy Bacon, Elizabeth Shepherd, Barbara Bell, Hannah Boothman, Sarah Boothman, Suzanne Parsons. Front row: Sally Musselwhite, Sherree Bell, Caroline Trueman, Carol Fielder.

mile from here to the back door of the Lodge then any telegrams were delivered free, but if they happened to be delivered to the front door then they were charged for!!

Every Thursday and Saturday a bus driven by Mr George Parsons left the village for Romsey, the fare being one shilling return. On one Thursday a month, for two shillings return, this same bus went to Southampton.

The Ex-Servicemen's Club hut, which later became the Social Club, was situated in the dell where Braishfield Garage stands. The recreation ground beside it had generously been given to the village by Mr King. There was always a very impressive turnout on Armistice Day with the men proudly displaying their medals marching to the War Memorial accompanied by the Braishfield Village Band.

Based on an article first published in the Braishfield Village News in 1983.

Dorothy Bacon was the daughter of Admiral Sir Reginald and Lady Bacon. Her father had a very distinguished naval career. Her brothers, Dudley and Robin, died young, the elder of war wounds in 1918 and the younger in the flu epidemic of 1919. They are both buried in the churchyard.

Miss Dorothy, as she was always known in the village, was the first secretary of the Braishfield Women's Institute. In 1938 she formed the 5th Hampshire ATS unit with fifty girls to do essential war work at home.

After the death of the Admiral, Lady Bacon and Miss Dorothy moved from Braishfield Lodge to Orchard Cottage in 1953. Always a generous benefactor to the village she was, among other things, Chairman of the Parish Council and President of the Horticultural Society. She retained a sharp interest in all aspects of village life until her death in 1998 at the age of ninety-one.

Vanished Buildings

1600–1980

Canister Cottage, Pucknall. The cottage stood to the left of Bramble Cottage in Dores Lane and was demolished in the 1950s. Miss Wheble, who is standing by the door, had been housekeeper at Farley Rectory in the 1930s to the Reverend Sidney Percival.

Cottages at the junction of Newport and Kiln Lanes in the 1950s just before they were demolished. In the late 1940s the Biddlecombe and Bristow families lived there. The Cottle family from the Newport Inn built their house 'Elttoc' on the site.

The Women's Institute Hall in 1967, taken from the entrance opposite April Cottage. All Saints' Church can be seen in the distance. The 'hut' was the hub of village activities, concerts and plays for over fifty years and the meeting place for the local WI, founded in 1921 by Lady Bacon. It was demolished in 1980 and the land sold by the WI to help pay for the new village hall which was opened in 1982. New houses Bryndlewood and Dellwood were built on the site.

The west side of the hut in the 1950s. The side door was used as an entrance in the summer. Left to right: Cyril Dunford, Millie Dunford, Joan Parsons and Bill Parsons who are attending a wedding reception.

The north wing of Woolley Green House. This eighteenth century farmhouse was extended in 1900; it had ten bedrooms, four attics and large cellars. In 1901 there was a staff of six, plus four gardeners and two coachmen. Miss Heathcote (formerly of Hursley Park), who lived at Woolley, was killed at the bricked-up entrance on Woolley Hill when a horse stepped on a pheasant, reared up and overturned the phaeton. Her ghost is supposed to ride down the hill annually on October 31st. Woolley was bought by the Cooper family at the turn of the century. The Butlers lived in the house for five years in the 1950s. It was bitterly cold in the winter but, because of the thick walls, cool in the summer.

This photograph from the Winchester Museum Collection is labelled 'Lower Braishfield'. Nothing resembling this scene exists in the village nor can anyone living here today identify its location. The most likely place is Pucknall along Dores Lane. It remains a mystery to us. Perhaps someone who reads this book can solve it.

The Braishfield Hoopmakers
Geoff Baird

1908–1921

A hurdle enclosure used for sheep shearing in the Braishfield Manor area during Mr King's time. Bill Randall's paternal grandfather is in the centre and his aunt, Lucy Randall, on the right. Sheep clippers were operated by a hand driven wheel with a flexible spindle.

Whilst hurdles are still a familiar sight in this part of the country and hurdlemakers, enjoying something of a revival thanks to the present day interest in gardening, still ply their craft as near at hand as Kings Somborne, the ancient woodland craft of barrel hoop making, once an important part of the woodcraft industry of the village of Braishfield, completely died out in the early 1920s.

The sole 'survivor' still living in the area of the twenty-five or so hoopmakers who were working in the woods and coppices, or in sheds around the village before the Great War, is our Sexton and Parish Clerk of All Saints' Braishfield, Mr Sidney Scorey. Mr Scorey's grandfather 'emigrated' to Braishfield from Durley well over a century ago, and brought with him the art of hoop bending, which he introduced into the local industry. Up to that time hoops had been sent to the coopers prepared, but straight, and had to be bent to conform with the shape of the barrel by the cooper himself as he applied them.

Successive generations of Scoreys followed the craft and, in 1908 when he was sixteen years of age, Sid Scorey, until then a garden boy at Hall Farm, Eldon, went to join his father in the trade in a copse near Michelmersh Church working for Mr Abrahams, who owned the village shop in The Square. Mr Abrahams would seem to have been the business organizer and financier of the local

Sid Scorey pictured in 1978 with the tools of his trade.

industry negotiating with landowners to buy the raw materials, hazel poles, arranging pole cutters and transport and the business of orders from and dispatch to customers.

Hoops were made in various sizes using poles from four feet six inches to ten feet in length though Mr Scorey can remember using fifteen-foot lengths for a short time. Bundles of completed hoops were kept at the working site until an order was received when they were picked up in horse drawn carts, taken to the railway station and dispatched by rail. Mr Scorey remembers that their entire production used to be sent to Staffordshire but does not know what the barrels of which they became a part were used for. For every thousand hoops ordered twelve hundred were supplied to allow for breakages.

Not all hoops were made in the woods. Poles were carted to various points around the village where hoop-makers had their huts. One Charles Cooper made hoops at Dummers (now Cromwell Cottage and Whites Cottage, Pucknall). Another hut stood near the site of the present rectory; and where Boares Garden now stands were several others.

To those of us who spend our lives in stuffy noisy offices at the mercy of the telephone all day their lives in the peace and tranquillity of the woods may seem to border on the idyllic, but it was, in truth, hard demanding work, poorly paid and exposed to all weathers. Mr Scorey says that for one bundle (ten gauges of six hoops) of the ten-foot size he was paid one shilling and threepence; for hogshead sizes of eight and nine feet, sixpence for a bundle of thirty. On an average day a hoopmaker could make four bundles of ten-foot hoops or seven bundles of hogshead size and could expect to earn about a pound a week. If he was sick – hard luck!

Mr Scorey left the village in 1915 to join the Royal Garrison Artillery, and when he returned from France in 1918 he found that hoopmaking had almost died out, having been super-seded by strip metal. He remembers, though, seeing them still being made in Sussex as he was passing through on a train journey in 1930.

Mr Scorey and his father Levi made the last hoop in Fairbourne Woods off Lower Street in 1921,

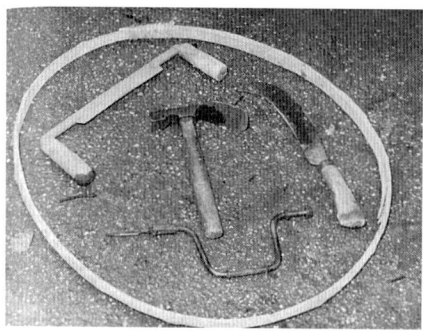

Some of the tools used in hoopmaking.

and another village industry passed into history.

The hoopmaking process

The hoop poles were cut and stacked in approximate lengths by cutters who went before the hoopmakers into the woods. The hoopmakers' first job was to set up the 'production line', possibly one of the earliest examples of what we think of as a modern innovation, and to build over it the framework of a rough shelter, which would be later roofed with shavings from the hoops as they were made.

A long horizontal rail was set up on posts a few feet from the ground at a convenient working height, partly to provide support for the 'jigs' (my term, not theirs) used in the production and partly to allow for the stacking of the hoops at the various stages of their passage down the production line. The efficiency and sound ergonomic principles governing the practices of the hoopmakers would provide a good example to many modern industrial firms. The process started on the left of the line where a bundle of untrimmed poles would be leaned against the rail. One end would then be trimmed square, the pole then reversed, with the trimmed end against a peg set in the ground at the exact distance from the top of a post set upright against the rail, as was required for the length of the hoop to be produced. The other end would then be cut off square at the correct length. The trimmed pole would then be transferred to the right hand side of the measuring stick and leaned against the rail to await the next stage of production.

When the whole bundle had been cut to length, the poles were split in half on a cutting rail using an adze and again transferred to the right for final trimming which was carried out on the 'pin post' as it was known. This was a substantial stake set upright in the ground **against** the horizontal rail which ran the length of the line. On the right hand side, and near the top of this stake, were inserted two wooden pegs, one above

A hazel copse.

the other, and about one half to three-quarters of an inch apart. One end of the, by now, split hoop pole was inserted between the horizontal pegs cut side uppermost, whilst the other end was supported in the grooved top of another stake set upright in the ground on the hoopmaker's side of the production line. The hoopmaker would then plane the flat side of the pole using a 'draw shave' a tool like a modern spokeshave only less refined, until the surface was uniformly flat, and suitable for application to the side of a barrel.

The next move to the right brought the hoop, now trimmed for length and surface, to the 'bending horse'. This was a section of round tree trunk or branch eight to ten inches in diameter held horizontally two and a half to three feet from the ground by four substantial legs. Parallel with the top of the trunk, and about a half inch above it, was fixed a light rail. The hoops were inserted between these two, bark side uppermost, and the maker, holding the hoop with his left hand and gradually feeding it between the rails, would push down on the part on the other side of the bending horse, moulding it approximately to the shape of the trunk which, stretching the fibres of the green wood, gave the hoop a permanent incurve.

Hoops were packed in half dozens, and the first of each six were drilled at the two ends, using a 'wimblepick' as it was known locally – a kind of simple brace and bit – and wooden pegs were inserted in the holes so that the hoop held its proper shape. Five others of the same size but unpegged were wound round inside the complete hoop, or 'gauge' as it was known, to keep them in rough shape. When ten gauges and their contents were completed they were stacked one on top of another on an inclined platform just off the ground called a 'packing board' and tied together with withies.

Based on an article first published in the Braishfield Village News in 1981.

Geoff Baird, a police officer serving at the Hampshire Police Headquarters at Winchester, moved with his family to Pucknall in 1976. Geoff and his wife, Audrey, soon became involved in village affairs. Geoff served on the PCC, the organising committee of the Braishfield Country Fair, as Chairman of the Village Association and as a member of the Twinning Committee. They moved from the village in 1984 and are now living in Somerset.

Our Lovely Village
Joan Bartlam

1959–1984

Church Lane in the 1930s taken from the garden of Orchard Cottage. The scene remained virtually unchanged until the first of the new houses was built in the early 1950s. The barn on the left is now Colsons Barn and beyond it is a car parked outside the entrance to The Cottage.

There have been many changes in Braishfield since we came to the village in 1959. Megana Way was just being developed, the first of about forty-eight new houses to be built, and many more houses have been altered beyond recognition.

There were very few cars then – this was when people walked to Romsey to shop (BW – Before Waitrose). Pearce's Bakery delivered bread three times a week, the greengrocer called and meat would be delivered by Stares, the butchers in Romsey. There were three shops in the village; they all seemed to thrive and were useful if you missed the bus.

Until the new village hall was built in 1979, all village business was conducted in the old WI Hut. It was the focus of village life, with meetings of the parish council, WI, etc. There were whist drives and best of all, wonderful concerts by the famous Braishfield Seven – they were all local girls (and boys to help with the lights, etc.) – Rita, Girlie, Joan, Shirley, Peggy, Janet and Mollie. Mrs Cottle played the piano. This was all local talent and village entertainment at its best.

There were three pubs. The jovial Alec Cottle was at The Newport, Jack Bailey at The Wheatsheaf and Mrs Monger at The Dog and Crook.

The 'Miss World' sketch from a Braishfield Seven concert in the 1960s in the WI Hall.

I was told that this pub was once thatched and some years ago a workman using a blowlamp set it on fire and all was burnt.

Until recently there were three well-known and respected personalities in Braishfield: Miss D Bacon, the Rev S Boothman (now Canon Boothman Retd) and Mrs E Shepherd, the headmistress at the village school, which was much smaller at that time.

About 1978 Braishfield staged a two day country fair at Pucknall Farm. People came from miles around, the traffic was nose to tail and the approach roads were blocked – it was incredible. Everything was there – bands, crafts, trade stalls, archery, Morris dancing, etc. We were featured on TV and written about in glowing terms. There was also a balloon and the farmer was taken up for a trip. As they took off, I remember some wag in the crowd shouted, "If you don't come back, we'll feed the cows!" (P.S. He did come back!)

Until a few years ago the hounds of the Hursley Hunt were kept at the kennels at Pucknall. They were often to be heard 'singing'. It was a lovely sight to see the hunt with master and hounds riding through the village – alas no more. Sometimes we would see a four-in-hand drive past. It would be driven by the famous George Abbott who told me he had driven the Queen's horses in London in ceremonial processions.

One day I saw a group of monks in long grey habits walking towards Winchester, perhaps on a pilgrimage. It seemed almost unreal as they walked past me completely silent – not even the sound of footsteps.

The mains drainage came in 1984 causing great upheaval. We were glad when it was finished.

The population seems to have been stable for years at about five hundred. I see on the Electoral Roll in 1976 it was four hundred and forty-five, 1982 – four hundred and ninety-two, 1999 – five hundred and nine. Over the years the constituency boundaries have changed. In 1960 we were in the Winchester Division, a few years later we were in the Eastleigh Division, then it was Romsey & Waterside – and now we are just Romsey Division.

Well, after all this, I must say I think Braishfield is a lovely village with lovely people and we would not like to live anywhere else. Let us pray that our village doesn't become any bigger.

Joan and Bill Bartlam moved from Ruislip in Middlesex to be in the country and bought a smallholding in Braishfield Road. When their son Roger married Rosemary the young couple took over the cottage and Bill and Joan moved to a bungalow close by. Joan worked actively for the Red Cross. She and Bill, both staunch Conservatives, were prominent organizers of the local party. Bill died, aged ninety-four, in 2003.

The hunt leaving the kennels in Dummers Road. Fred Gosden is the huntsman.

The Evacuee
Anne Beggs

1940

I was ten when I came to Braishfield from Gosport because there were bombs dropping where I lived. You really didn't have much of a chance to be frightened except when you said goodbye to your parents. There were forty-five of us that came from Brocas Junior School in Aybury Lane and when we got here there were people waiting in the school to take us. I went to this lady who actually turned out to be really nice but the first thing she said to me was, "Oh, I really wanted somebody older", and that rather put me off because I thought she didn't want me, but she did. Her name was Mrs Quick and she lived in Newport Lane. I had a nice little bedroom in her tiny cottage. There wasn't a bathroom and you had to go right down the garden to a little hut for the lavatory. I didn't like the idea of spiders and other things down there so I never went out at night.

I was an only child and had hoped to go to a home where there were other children because it would be fun but I was just with this lady whose husband had been killed in the First World War. Her family had Malthouse Farm and we used to walk to it across the fields in the evening. We collected twigs and small branches for her stove on which she cooked all our meals. There was a huge walnut tree in a field on our

Anne Frost in her school uniform in 1941, the year after her stay in Braishfield.

Mrs Annie Quick (born Parsons) in later life outside her cottage, now known as Annie's Cottage, in Newport Lane.

23

Jim Parsons with son, Stan, and Stan's friend, John Mason at Malthouse Farm.

route and in the autumn we picked up the fallen nuts. During the War you couldn't get much meat because food was rationed. The farmer, Mr Jim Parsons, used to shoot pheasants so I had pheasant for the first time in my life. Living at the farm there was a boy from Gosport, Ronald Kidd, and I played with him and the farmer's son, Stan.

At harvest time we went to the fields and the men shot rabbits as they ran out of the wheat. I hated that. When the mushrooms were growing we collected them with Mr Parsons' family. They used to fill tin baths with them. Some were as big as dinner plates and were called horse mushrooms. I think they sold them at the market. In those days fields were not subject to spraying so mushrooms grew in great profusion. We went to church every Sunday and I was allowed to play at a farm near there after school. I used to sit on a big carthorse. The farmer cooked vegetables on a stove in his yard which he fed to the pigs.

My father came to visit me here two or three times on his bicycle but I can't remember whether he cycled from Gosport or whether he put his bike on the train and got off at Romsey. He used to smoke cigarettes and Mrs Quick wouldn't let him smoke in the house so we went into the garden.

W G Owen with one of his pigs at Elm Grove.

I recall being cast in a school play as French chef. I had to wear my stockings tucked into my knickers – I was mortified! But I enjoyed the village school and I am sure my education was improved during my time there. We played a game, stoolball*, which I had never encountered before – or since.

One time there were people playing in the recreation ground when Mrs Quick and I were walking past along the road and this German plane came over and started to machine gun. We dived into the ditch as he flew over the recreation ground. He was probably just frightening people but there were definitely bullets flying around. Nobody was hurt so either he didn't want to kill anybody or he wasn't a very good shot. The roads around the village were full of soldiers and their vehicles. We all chatted to the men, and the women took them tea and any treats they could find. Of course, the children thought it was all exciting and great fun. We didn't know what was awaiting the men on the other side of the Channel.

I went back home just for Christmas but didn't come back again because I persuaded my parents to let me stay at home with them. In 1997 I met again Girlie Old and Rita Stitt. Rita remembered me at school. Girlie was a landgirl and she drove a small car and used to give the locals lifts to Romsey. I only went there twice because it was a long walk from Braishfield.

Anne Beggs (born Anne Frost) was evacuated to Braishfield in 1940 and stayed for six months. The memory above was extracted from a transcript of a question and answer session with the children at Braishfield School during a visit she made to the village in July 1997.

* stoolball – an ancient Sussex game, the first reference to it was written in the fifteenth century. Milking stools were used by the maids as wicket and, the legs having been removed, bat. The game survives, played by women and girls in the main, in its home county. The foot square, head height wooden targets, standing on four legs, are set sixteen yards apart. With two batsmen, a small ball and much the same rules as our summer game it is often described as 'cricket in the air'.

Twinning with Crouay
Barbara Bell

1977–2000

Barbara Bell and the Mayor of Crouay, Jacques Letourneur, by the village twinning sign in Crouay.

I was involved with the Braishfield/Crouay twinning right from its inception in 1977 since I was, at that time, Chairman of the Parish Council, although it was Simone and Roy Hughes who were the prime movers. The first approach was made by the Mayor of Crouay, Jacques Letourneur. When he had the idea of a village twinning, a new concept at that time, he mentioned it to his neighbour, William, who just happened to be Simone's nephew.

It soon became apparent that there was quite a difference between being the mayor of a French village and an English parish council chairman. Jacques could levy and collect rates, or their French equivalent, and had many advantages over his English counterpart – for instance, Crouay owned the school bus, a great help with twinning visit transport. The gîtes were very useful supplementary accommodation. The Mayor also had the Salle des Fêtes at his disposal; whereas Braishfield had no village hall until January 1982. We were welcomed so warmly on our first visit that we wondered how we could possibly afford to repay such hospitality! The Braishfield Twinning Committee had to rely on fundraising events to provide every penny spent on our guests. But we all made a great effort and successfully entertained them inspired by the spirit of friendship and goodwill.

Many of us have made real friendships over the years; Brigitte, Jacques Letourneur's eldest daughter, came to live and work in England and stayed with us for some time before moving to Romsey.

A great boost to the twinning was given by the enthusiasm of the football club, led by their chairman, Bill Henderson – then landlord of the Wheatsheaf – and their captain, Dave Leigh. On one memorable occasion the village and the football club made a combined visit which meant that, with our French hosts, more than sixty of us sat down to the Saturday evening meal. Organising that weekend was quite a challenge to the powers of even Jacques Letourneur.

Our twinning differed from most such arrangements in another respect; this was our joint observance, every year, of Armistice Day. For many years, there were Braishfield representatives at the Crouay ceremony which was held on November 11th itself and they came to us on the nearest Sunday to that date – so that we did not have to be in two places at once! Both national flags are still displayed and both lists of the fallen read at the services on each side of the Channel.

The schools, I am delighted to say, still arrange visits. No other official exchanges now take place, although there are still many personal connections. I am very glad to have been part of our twinning venture and look back on my memories of so many happy occasions with gratitude.

Crouay twinning dinner in the village hall. Seated, far left, Bill Grundy. Standing, left to right, Roy Hughes, Simone Hughes, Jacques Letourneur, Barbara Bell.

The first visit to Crouay in April 1977. The group is pictured outside the Mairie. Left to right: Jill Samways, Geoff Baird, Susie Donnelly, Audrey Baird, Mike Samways, William Glover, Ann Bird, John Saunders, Peggy Parsons, Alan Smith, Simone Hughes, Shirley Smith, Jim Stewart, Ian Baird, Rusty Smith, Stan Parsons. At the far right is M Letourneur, the father of the mayor.

Barbara Bell came to Braishfield in 1954 with her husband, Douglas, and children, Jim and Patsy, intending to become a part of the life of a small village and to keep chickens. They bought Meadow Cottage in Newport Lane and with it the piece of land on which they later built Potters Clay. Barbara was a leading member of the WI, a founder member of the Twinning Committee and a prime instigator and fundraiser in the building of the village hall, acting as Chairman of the Hall Management Committee for many years. An active member of All Saints' Church she was a churchwarden and served on the PCC. They moved to Dorset in 2001.

A Rector's Perspective
Samuel Boothman

1946–1981

Samuel and Mary Boothman receiving a presentation in March 1971 from Braishfield Parochial Church Council to mark their twenty-five years in the parish. Also present are Dorothy Bacon (vice-chairman), George Parsons and Douglas Lowman (churchwardens).

When we came to Braishfield in 1946 it seemed as if the village was at the end of an era. Until the Second World War the three big houses, the Manor, the Lodge and Braishfield House, each had a full retinue of staff, mostly drawn from the people of the village and all the farms had a good number of employees. The system lingered; one caught a glimpse of it from those who were inclined to talk about the time when relatively few worked outside the village.

Mr and Mrs King had enlarged the original manor farmhouse with its Georgian façade by adding a billiard room to the right and a drawing room to the left presenting the impressive front of the Manor as we see it now. While it was said that Mr King was rather retiring, Mrs King had been the 'lady of the manor', often presiding over and encouraging village activities. She had her own stud of ponies and competed successfully as a hackney carriage driver. When the Kings departed several of the farms owned by the Manor were sold. A number of former staff found work outside the village; Fred Chapman and Tom Ross gained employment with Strongs of Romsey. Properties were increasingly acquired by people coming to settle in the village, some to retire and some whose occupations

Charlie Saunders outside Yew Tree Cottage in 1946. He gardened for the Boothmans and 'blew' (pumped) the pipe organ at All Saints' Church. He lived at 3 Pond Cottages.

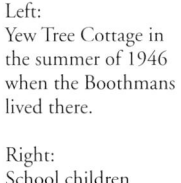

Left:
Yew Tree Cottage in the summer of 1946 when the Boothmans lived there.

Right:
School children dancing on the Rectory lawn in the 1960s at a Church Bring and Buy Sale. The house is now a private residence called Seven Pines.

took them as far afield as Winchester and Southampton.

My predecessors, the Reverend Sydney Percival and the Reverend Woodham Waddilove, had resided at Farley Rectory which was sold during the war. We lived in the village of Braishfield itself and were warmly welcomed and in turn I was impressed by the wonderful community spirit. There were three shops and the three public houses. The Social Club, whose headquarters was opposite the chapel, was well supported.

Our first home was at Yew Tree Cottage in Church Lane. On Saturday nights we heard the dances in the Women's Institute Hut. As the hut stood on brick piers on the sloping site, the vibrations from the wooden floor were quite loud! The old Vicarage, renamed The Close, had been sold in 1928 when the ecclesiastical parish was combined with Farley. Plans to build a new rectory after the war took some years to come to fruition. It was a very difficult time because of the severe shortage of building materials and many families had to wait for accommodation. We moved up to Spinney Corner on a two-year lease in 1947. Kind parishioners assisted us with the move. I remember my books being transported up Church Lane in a wheelbarrow by Charlie Saunders who worked in the garden at Yew Tree Cottage! Eventually we spent eighteen months living in Winchester at St Thomas's Rectory with my father-in-law, Canon George Uppington, before we moved into the new rectory in September 1950. The land was very kindly given by Mrs Heuston and the two parishes raised part of the money for

From CROOK HILL

To FARLEY MOUNT

OCCASIONAL NOTES & NOTICES FOR THE PARISHES OF
FARLEY CHAMBERLAYNE & BRAISHFIELD

Norman Thelwell, who lived in the village, designed the cover of the church magazine and made the woodcuts of the two churches.

the house which was restricted in size due to the planning regulations of the time. I have been told that the field, called Daisyfield, used to be the site of the annual Trinity Monday Fair. A year or two later new houses were built on the south side of Hill View and families were able to move into much longed for homes.

As Chairman of the Managers I was closely involved with the school. Miss Margaret Euston was a fine secondary schoolteacher who had taken the position of headmistress to provide a home for her widowed mother at the schoolhouse. The 1944 Education Act was to bring radical change; from the mid-fifties the children went to Romsey for their secondary education. When the new kitchen was built the children had the nourishment of freshly prepared food; previously meals were delivered in containers. Mrs Teece, another dedicated headmistress, followed and she was succeeded by Mrs Elizabeth Shepherd, also dedicated, strict, fair and very resourceful.

Major General Ransome was instrumental in gaining for Braishfield the status of civil parish, resulting in the formation of Braishfield Parish Council in 1951. Until then the village affairs were administered from Michelmersh.

The community spirit of the village was demonstrated by the activities of the Braishfield Seven whose shows became ever more popular. These took place in the WI Hut. In the late 1960s fundraising for Christian Aid began with a coffee morning at the Rectory, supported by the then Congregational Chapel. This quickly developed into a full week of fundraising activities arranged by many village groups and organisations, including the pubs and the cricket and football teams. This was a remarkable example of the way in which everyone in the village works together for a common cause.

The Reverend Canon Boothman was Rector of the Parishes of Farley Chamberlayne and Braishfield from 1946 to his retirement in 1981. Five times a year between 1960 and 1981 he produced a letter to parishioners entitled 'From Crookhill to Farley Mount – Occasional Notes and Notices for the Parishes of Farley Chamberlayne and Braishfield'. The following two extracts are taken from this publication.

The interior of All Saints' Church in 1975 decorated for the wedding of Jane Snow to Richard Kay.

September 1963

During the unusually severe cold of last winter we were buoyed up by the hope that a really good summer would follow. The cool wet summer we have had has brought many disappointments; but few can have experienced a disappointment equal to that which the farmers are experiencing this autumn. Last winter the farming community battled through arctic conditions to ensure that the daily milk supplies were maintained and that animals were fed and watered. Now the season of harvest is with us, and it is with trying conditions of another sort that the farmer is contending, crops of good promise are being harvested late and with great difficulty.

Although we are a country parish, relatively few of our parishioners are now engaged in the work of agriculture; but to those who are so engaged we can at least shew that we are aware of the fact that their difficulties are great and, at the same time, express the hope that their labours will be rewarded with good success.

The services of thanksgiving for the harvest are announced for early October; we hope that by then the grain crops will have been gathered. However it is not only for the golden grain that we give thanks at harvest – but also for all the crops and fruits of the year which provide food for man and beast. We also remember that through our imports from overseas we receive a share of the harvests of the world.

November 1966

When the centenary of the consecration of Braishfield Church was celebrated in March 1955 we recorded in a special leaflet some of the details known about its building: viz – that the chief promoter and benefactor of the scheme was The Reverend James Davies of Braishfield House; that the builder was Mr John Petty of Wellow and that the seating was made by Mr Wheeler of Romsey. Mention was also made of certain people in the area who had helped the people of Braishfield to provide a parish church for the village. But unfortunately no reference could be made to the architect who designed the church as contemporary accounts had omitted to mention his name.

However on various occasions I myself have endeavoured to pay tribute to this unknown architect for the simple but well-proportioned interior of the building which derives its restful atmosphere from the skilful use of plain wall surfaces broken by deep-set windows and simple arcading, supported by round stone pillars; the whole composition relying for its architectural effect upon the inter-

Left: All Saints' Church from Church Lane prior to 1902 when the turret and clock tower were added. All Saints' was consecrated on Thursday 15th March 1855.

Right: All Saints' Church clock tower was added in 1902 to celebrate the Coronation of King Edward VII.

play of light and shade which varies according to the time of day. Another feature which is worthy of note is the gradual ascent from the porch to the altar – never more than one step at a time.

I have always attributed the pleasing simplicity of the building to the fact that cost must have been a deciding factor and that because of this we were spared the elaborate ornamentation which was characteristic of the latter half of the nineteenth century. It had not occurred to me that the building might have been designed by one of the leading church architects of the day.

Recently an author who is preparing a new biography of William Butterfield (1814–1900) wrote from the University of Essex to ask if by any chance we had amongst our church records any letters or papers from William Butterfield who was the designer of Braishfield Church. He was also the architect for several London churches and Keble College, Oxford. I replied to say that regretfully we had no such papers but that I was more than grateful for the information he had given me. So now we know what at one time we thought we would never know!

I hope that many will look again at the interior of Braishfield Church with renewed appreciation of a building which despite its almost severe simplicity has an atmosphere of devotion and quiet which makes it one of the pleasantest of places in which to join in the prayers and praises of the church.

It was not for the sake of ornamentation that part of the fourth verse of Psalm 100 was inscribed over the door – "Enter into his gates with thanksgiving and into his courts with praise" – one has but to step inside the church to become aware of the part that William Butterfield has played in giving to the people of Braishfield a place of devotion and quiet where they can find, through the years, the grace of God to sustain them in "all the changing scenes of life".

Sam Boothman grew up on a farm just south of Dublin, one of seven children. After studying at Trinity College Dublin his first curacy was at Enniskillen. A second curacy followed at St Michael and St Thomas, Winchester, where the rector was Canon George Uppington whose daughter, Mary, Sam married in 1946. During the war Sam had been an Army Chaplain. He was rector of the United Benefice of Farley Chamberlayne with Braishfield until his retirement in 1981. For the last eighteen months of his incumbency the benefice was extended to include Michelmersh and Timsbury. Now aged ninety-three he lives in retirement in Ampfield with his daughters, Hannah and Sarah.

The Braishfield School Log Books
Ann Chant

1877–1899

Braishfield School in the late 1800s. The schoolhouse is on the right. The north end of the school on the left has disappeared after later additions to the building.

On the 14th May 1877 Braishfield Public Elementary School opened its doors for the first time to receive thirty-eight boys, girls and infants. The village was very much a farming community and, as such, both parents' and children's lives were ruled by the seasonal requirements of the farms they worked on and, of course, the weather.

The cost of schooling in 1877 was one penny a week. The average farm labourer's wage in 1906 was twelve to fifteen shillings a week and a shepherd earned sixteen to eighteen shillings a week. It was often a struggle to feed, clothe and send children to school.

2nd November 1877
The children have attended much better this week. Today I had 48 children which is the highest number I have had altogether. The Rev. J. Durrant visited this school Tuesday and Thursday. Mrs. Durrant kindly sent me some thimbles for the little ones. Admitted Harriet Sivier at a 1d per week. Taught the children a new song "The Hare" and a new evening hymn.
B. Fryer.

The Old Family outside 1 Fairbourne Cottages in 1902. Left to right: Back row: Frederick Old, Ernest Old, Ethel Old, Lily Old (Proom – June Thomson's mother), George Old, Walter Old (Reg 'Boxer' Old's father). Front row: Charles and Emma Old (parents), May Old (Bill Parsons' mother) on her father's knee, Emma Old (Joyce Alford's mother) at her mother's knee. Percival Old (Rita Stitt's father) is missing from the photo.

22nd February 1878
There has been somewhat a falling off in the attendance this week. Catherine Webb has been kept away, her father refusing to pay the 2d fee charged by the Board.

Severe weather often prevented the children from attending school and good boots were essential for walking along muddy and unmetalled roads.

21st January 1881
The school has been closed since Tuesday last on account of the unusually heavy fall of snow so keeping the children at home.

16th January 1891
A pleasing circumstance took place one day this week, shewing "British determination" to overcome difficulty. Three children (The Olds) started to come to school. As it was more than usually slippery down their road, they tried to protect their feet from slipping by tying haybonds round their boots. When these wore off, they found they had the worst part to come over, and, as they found themselves <u>unable to walk</u> over the sheet of ice composing the surface for many yards, they <u>crawled</u> over it, rather than go back home.

Braishfield School early in the twentieth century (postcard franked Romsey March 18, 1906). The sapling is now a splendid oak tree but the bell tower has vanished. The schoolchildren are assembled by the entrance. The schoolhouse, seen on the left, was demolished in the 1990s to allow for extension of the school buildings.

March 11th 1891
This morning 7 children appeared, and were sent home again, as they were wet through at the boots from snow-water soaking through. No school held. The roads in several parts of the village have been completely blocked with snow-drifts. Men at work clearing passages for vehicular traffic.

May 13th 1892
Good attendance throughout the week – Average 102. School work (with the exception of the usual slow-coaches) has been well done. Some children talked to about coming to school with "rusty" boots – today and yesterday. There was a great improvement in the appearance of the boots this morning; almost every child's boots had been polished. Marks promised for clean boots.

May 16th 1892
91 children present this morning:- 88 pairs of clean boots.

January 31st 1896
The school was used (by Board's consent) last evening by the Big Chapel Temperance Band of Hope who gave a 'Magic Lantern Entertainment' (free) to the children who are members, and made a charge of 2d for the adults. Almost the whole time there was a disgraceful noise, with feet, which was accompanied with shouting. Master heard the noise almost ¾ mile off. The smaller Desks (used by the First Standard) are damaged much by the friction with the <u>Fourteen year old men's hob-nailed understandings.</u>

Children were required to help their parents on the land. Absences were often registered due to the necessity of helping with planting, harvesting, haymaking or nut gathering.

3rd August 1877
All of the elder children have gone to assist their parents in the harvest fields. Broke up today for harvest holidays.

1891

Jan? to prolonged severe weather.

9th — School closed to-day, owing to Master having to attend his mother's burial at Alton

15th Mr Mintrum (Attendance Officer) visited this afternoon

omitted 12th Miss Way and Miss E. Way visited this afternoon.

16th Average for the week 52.5. Several children absent with "Bad Colds":— many still away on account of severe weather.

A pleasing circumstance took place one day this week, shewing "British determination" to overcome difficulty:— "Three children — ("The Olds") — started to come to school. As it was more than usually slippery down their road, they tried to protect their feet from slipping

Pages from the School Log Books of January 1891.

by ~~tied~~ tying haybonds round their boots. When these wore off, they found they had the worst part to come over; and, as they found themselves unable to walk over the sheet of ice composing the surface for many yards, — they crawled over it, rather than go back home.

Jany. 20th Emily Dewey, (who has been absent from school for a considerable time, — through sickness) was removed to the "Infirmary" to-day.

Ella Wort, one of the most irregular children on the Books, returned to school.

23rd Average for the week 55.9. Many away from colds: but more unable to come through inclement weather, & slippery roads.

Children, on the whole, seem making good progress.

(22nd) Copy of Geo. Abraham's Sum; — boy too idle to try :— = 93647 × 780
  780
 3030470
  514470.

Braishfield School group in 1914. Known faces: Daisy, Lily and Robert Old.

5th October 1877
No better attendance again this week, many are away nut gathering. They seem to imagine that they can stay away from school when they think proper to do so. Examined each Standard alternately in arithmetic.

28th June 1878
The attendance this week has been better in the lower classes, but in the first class many of the boys are very irregular owing to haymaking. Henry Jerrum has been away with a bad hand this last two weeks. Also William Goulding has this week hurt his hand with a machine and has been kept away in consequence.

21st May 1883
There being a Fete in the village today the attendance was only 27. The school was closed this afternoon.

22nd June 1883
Many of the elder children being at work in the fields haymaking the average this week is only 75.3.

9th July 1883
The attendance this morning was only 57 and this afternoon 47, many of the children being at the Chapel Sunday School Treat.

On *27th October 1884* attendance was "but 40, many of the children being away picking up acorns."

April 24th 1891
One or two away on sick list: also several away part of week "planting potatoes". Children strictly warned about "stone-throwing" when going home from school.

* a small faggot or bundle of firewood.

May 1st 1891
Several children absent throughout the week (or very irregular) being illegally employed.

16th June 1892
Mr. C. Mintrum (Attendance Officer) called this morning. Two boys William Whitmarsh and Frederick Dewey warned by him, that they must not go to lead horses in the hay-field.

November 21st 1892
N.B. The two Elder children are being very handy to their parents – the boy "helping to make pimps"* and the girl "minding the baby", while the mother does a large amount of washing.

The summer school holiday was known as Harvest Holiday and in 1896 was for four weeks.

8th July 1877
A very thin attendance the whole of this week, harvest having commenced in some parts of the neighbourhood and the children are kept away to assist their parents.

22nd September 1879
Monday – School work re-commenced today the holidays having been prolonged to five weeks on account of the late harvest. Only 30 children have come back this morning.

26th September 1879
Average has not improved for the week it being 34, owing to the harvest being still uncompleted.

24th August 1896
School re-opened this (Monday) morning after Harvest Holiday of 4 weeks.

June 21st 1898
Attendance very slack in the Higher Standards owing to haymaking.

Outbreaks of illnesses were taken very seriously and the school would be closed.

22nd Sept. 1879
The School was re-opened today after the Harvest Holidays which were unavoidably extended because of the measles.

The pupils of Braishfield School in the first decade of the twentieth century.

Lily Old's good attendance certificate, dated 1907, when she was eleven years old. Lily married Bertram Proom.

Hampshire County Council.
EDUCATION COMMITTEE.
This is to Certify
That Lily Old 11 years of age, a Scholar at the Braishfield Council School, has during the School year ended 31st March 1907 made at least 400 Attendances.

A. L. Porter — For the Managers.
C. H. Carpenter — Head Teacher.
David Cowan — Director of Education.

July 22nd 1892
Nine children away "sick":- four with bad throats, 1 Scarlet Fever, 1 with bad twist of neck through a fall, 1 with Jaundice.

October 12th 1892
School closed by Order of Doctor, on account of Prevalence of Scarlet Fever in village, amongst children. Average for the 3 days = 62.3. No. on Books = 114. Present at all = 73. Absent all 3 days = 41 (mostly on account of sickness).

November 21st 1892
School re-opened this morning (by Doctor's permission) after being shut between five and six weeks. Present in morning only 59. Master sent out notes asking for "Reasons" of children's absence:- some very novel sent: e.g. "I was afraid the School would not be aired"! Present in afternoon: 73. One message in reply to note – "I baint going to send them, as I be afeard they'll catch summat"!

Sept. 14th 1893
Inquest held this evening, at 6.30 on Cause of Death of Henry C. Grace – a Standard IV boy of 11 years of age – who died on Monday last. Master on jury – Verdict: Death from Misadventure – caused by eating poisonous berries.

Sept. 15th 1893
No school this afternoon – owing to burial of Henry Grace's body.

Sept. 25th 1893
Annie Withers died this morning at 4.30, and her little baby sister on Saturday morning last: both from Diphtheria. Several other children absent with 'Bad Throat'. School closed this afternoon by order of Dr. F. Buckell (Medical Officer of Health) owing to several cases of Diphtheria in parish.

24th April 1896
The three children "Vane" absent all the week as the youngest (Lizzie) is suffering with "Measles".

1st May 1896
…several children away from school part of the week suffering from eruption, which looks very much like "Chicken-Pox".

6th May 1896
Mr. Dawkins, Sanitary Inspector, called to get names of children absent from Measles and Chicken Pox.

23rd November 1896
School re-opened for work this morning after a closure of 5 weeks. Attendance 57 a.m., 61 p.m. Still a great many unable to come, but nearly every family of children has had the Epidemic in their midst.

24th December 1896
School broke up this noon for Xmas holidays which, this year, are to be shorter than usual owing to school being closed for Epidemic some time since.

April 15th 1897
Katie Fielder absent whole week and part of last on account of Parent having slight attack of Diphtheria.

October 17th & 18th 1898
Several children away with Whooping cough.

January 10th 1899
There are six cases of Diphtheria in one house in the village and two more of Influenza. Children are in some cases kept away for fear of infection, although the families concerned are rigidly excluded from School Attendance.

These extracts are from the Victorian Log Books kept at the Hampshire Record Office. They are available to the public for reference and contain much of social and historical interest. The selections were made by Ann Chant, a retired teacher, who moved to the village with her husband, Tony, in 1987.

School

1923–2003

Braishfield County School, probably around 1923. Known faces: Back row: Lily Old. Second row: Rosie Miles, Edna Moss. Third row: Mary Moss. Front row: George Miles (in sailor suit).

Braishfield School girls in 1947. Left to right: Back row: Margaret Fielder, Audrey Sweet, Rosemary Thorne, Eileen Pritchard, Margaret Pritchard, Heather Foxcroft, Ann Goulding. Fourth row: Rona Bristow, Joan Parsons, Pamela Elkins, Yvonne Love, Pat Hyde, Pamela Gritt, Sylvia Chapman. Third row: Elsie Holey, Heather Webb, June Biddlecombe, Shirley Cottle, Sheila Carpenter, Ella Sweet, Hazel Ward. Second row: Irene Fielder, Hazel Watts, Shirley Bristow, Rita Biddlecombe, Pat ?, June Ward, Ann Allen. Front row: Pauline Reed, Leslie Greenwood, Rosemary Barfoot, Jean Head, Valerie Bailey, Beryl Bristow, Elizabeth Benham.

A visit from the police to Braishfield School in 1981. The temporary infants classroom behind was replaced by a classroom and office extension, and the new music room opened in 2003.

The pupils and staff of Braishfield School in 2003.

The Square in Norman Thelwell's Time
Tony Chant

1959–1969

When Norman and Rhona Thelwell moved to Braishfield in 1959 pictures of their houses, Church View (now Cherry Hill), and Rose Cottage (now Amberley) showed a very different scene from that which presents itself today. They were clearly welcomed by the villagers, and some of their contemporaries have very fond memories of the family. It is worth quoting one or two extracts from Norman's autobiography.

"When we took over the place was known as Church View. We planted flowering cherry trees by the gate and changed its name to Cherry Hill. It proved a happy place to live and work and our children were very happy there too. As we pushed ahead with clearing-up operations we amassed large quantities of wood which was no longer sound enough to be used again, and from time to time we had bonfires. Sometimes they were just a family affair with everyone sitting around them as dusk fell and eating toffee apples, but sometimes we held off until my brother came down with Cath and their children. The most memorable bonfire took place on the 5th November 1960". Thelwell goes on to describe a Guy Fawkes party which got totally out of hand. He recalls that, not wishing to appear parsimonious, he perhaps overdid the fireworks… "By the time things got under way, we had an embarrassment of explosives and it became clear to us fathers that we were all going to be needed to apply matches to the blue paper if we were going to get through it all. I think the first hint of panic swept over me when there were six rockets in the sky at the same time!" The present owners of Cherry Hill and Amberley had a similar fireworks party to see in the new Millennium. I suspect this pyromania goes with the house.

Norman and Rhona Thelwell.

Rose Cottage, front view, in 1960. Orchard Lodge and Orchard Cottage can be seen in the background.

When Thelwell bought Cherry Hill two semi-detached cottages were included in the package, one of which was named Rose Cottage. They were occupied by a man and wife on one side and a mother and two teenaged children on the other. The cottages really weren't in a particularly good state of repair according to Norman. He goes on to say, "They were like so many run down cottages which existed all over the countryside after the Second World War, however, they were picturesque and added a good deal of visual charm to that part of the village." But the facts were grim. "The roof was rotten and leaking, the walls were damp. Two earth closets outside catered for sanitation. The dwellings consisted of one room upstairs and one down, connected by small spiral staircases tucked into the corner of the building. Each cottage had a lean-to wooden shed with a tap which, together with electric light, were the only signs of convenience. There was no question of us profiting in any way by owning these cottages but technically we were the landlords and it caused us considerable anguish. Both families had lived in the building for many years and it was difficult to know how to act without seeming either to be interfering with their privacy or to be indifferent to their plight."

He then goes on to describe how the families were re-housed and he began to take the building down. The local builders were clearly not too keen to get involved. He adds, "We were much relieved when the two families were re-housed and the authorities issued a demolition order on the cottages. But if I sat by and watched them fall to the bulldozers the character of that part of the village would change overnight and I could not visualise another house which would fit into its surroundings so well. I needed time to think so I asked for a stay of execution and was given a year's grace to come up with a solution and of course the solution was the best part of the house which is now called Amberley…" Norman and Rhona felt it was so beautiful they decided to move into it and to lease out Cherry Hill.

Newcomers like Norman, although made welcome, were also considered by the old villagers as being part of the problem. He quotes a villager as follows: " 'That's the trouble, you see,' he would say, 'These people come along and buy up our homes and there's nothing left for the likes of us.' " He comments that there was no rancour in the man and that he always remained on excellent terms with him but it was quite obvious that the Thelwells were regarded as being privileged.

Several years later the Thelwells moved to Timsbury but still kept up with their friends and contacts within the village. Much of what has been related above is confirmed by people who knew him, like the Bartlams and the Birds and, indeed, Bernard Cook at the Newport Inn.

So here we have a generation of people now in their late seventies and early eighties who were extremely active in the village in the 1950s and 1960s. They talk of hedges being kept much higher and tidier. They were all in thrall to Miss Bacon. One of the sad memories of Mr and Mrs Bartlam was of seeing Miss Bacon's various effects for sale at the auction shortly after she died in 1998 which included the feathers she had worn in her tiara when being presented at Court. They also recall that Norman Thelwell could have bought the land backing onto the church paddock, and much regretted that he didn't. The new houses built lower down the road were a great annoyance to him over the years.

Some people dressed up and 'posh people' dressed down. Mr Joe Miller of Merrie Meade Farm used to go round in a big Bentley giving people lifts. General Ransome, on the other hand, dressed down, going round in an old coat tied up with string. The wife of the same Joe Miller of Merrie Meade advertised for a cook general (I guess, in today's terms, a housekeeper). Not long after, she found General Ransome on her doorstep who introduced himself as "general (someone or other)" and assumed he was applying for the job. She immediately took him in and offered the position to the startled General, showing him what she needed cooking!

Finally, of course, nothing really changes. Even then there were planning disputes, resentment of new buildings, village societies formed by a cross section of all villagers, and three active pubs. In other words a dynamic small society trying to make

Braishfield Road looking south with Rose Cottage, now called Amberley, on the right. The Square can be seen in the distance. The white gate on the left leads to Orchard Lodge. The four children are sitting on the bank of Daisyfield where the annual Trinity Monday Fair was held. The postcard is franked 17th October 1907.

sense of all the changes going on around them … just like now.

The above is based on Norman's published recollections, with reminiscences from his friends, Bill and Joan Bartlam and Bert and Anne Bird. The quotes are from Wrestling with a Pencil, **by Norman Thelwell (Methuen, London 1987).**

Norman and Rhona Thelwell lived in the village with their children, David and Penny, until 1969 when they moved to Timsbury.

Farmers and Farming
Janet Cook

as told to Tony Chant

1941–1950

Fifty years ago the pattern of farming in Braishfield was very different from that of today. For a start the village had two 'lengthmen', George Musslewhite and Bill Gritt, employed full time repairing hedges and clearing ditches. Stock was moved through the lanes from field to field and everyone made sure that they had a gate to block their garden entrance to protect their flowers, fruit and vegetables! Some villagers, for instance Tom Martin, kept their own animals. Tom had a cow he tethered in the verges wherever the grazing was best. There were rows of men in the fields hoeing. This style of farming has now largely been replaced. Cattle feed mostly on silage and far fewer vegetables are grown. Indeed it is doubtful that dairy farming as such will survive locally.

Towards the end of the First World War council land was given, fifty acres at a time together with a house,

Janet Cook, wearing her Easter bonnet, and Ken Smith at the Newport Inn in 1998.

Hall Place, south side, in 1961.

51

A tractor and binder at Hall Place during the war. Raymond Butler is on the tractor.

Mr Pitts on his horse at Fairbournes Farm before the war. He farmed there from 1935 to 1946.

to enable people to be self-supporting. Later, during the Second World War, the Ministry of Agriculture provided a common store of equipment such as ploughs and harrows for all to use. As well as dairy and cattle there was much arable land. Crops even included daffodils. Labourers picking stones off the fields often mistook stones for daffodil bulbs which is why you see so many growing along the edges of certain fields in the spring.

Some of the farms around the village have been owned by the same family for generations while others have changed hands, sometimes several times, during the last fifty years. There were a number of smallholdings and farms around Braishfield and names like the Harris family at Malthouse Farm and the Corrys at Pucknall Farm, where the Braishfield Country Fair was held, all played their part. A great deal of sugar beet was grown; we even had a 'sugar beet special train' from Romsey station! The Sheppards at **Hall Place** grew blackcurrants.

Crook Hill Farm was owned by Major General Cuthbertson who also had **Paynes Hay Farm** at that time. He lived in Ampfield House before moving to Braishfield House. Crook Hill Farm has now been incorporated into the Hilliers estate and was farmed by Peter Baker. Mr W G Owen farmed **Elm Grove Farm** in the centre of the village. 'Billy' Owen's daughter, Mrs Hoddinott, took over and her son, Michael, is still there. Johnnie Goulding, Jess Wells and Reg and George Randall worked there, as did Girlie Old. Some of these farm workers lived in Pond Cottages, the thatched cottages half way through the village. **Paynes Hay Farm** in Lower Street was a large mixed farm years ago and is now mostly arable. It is now farmed by Mr and Mrs John Oliphant, but for many years it was owned by the Vincent family. Gordon and Charlie Parsons worked there … the Parsons were said to be "very fine woodsmen". **Pitt Farm** on the Kings Somborne Road was farmed by Dover Dance who also had a cattle haulage business. The Willett family who eventually moved to the West Country followed him. Then under Billy Hebblethwaite it started producing vegetables employing many villagers in the process during harvest.

Fairbourne Farm was farmed by Mr Pitts who was also in the Home Guard, followed by Mr Cook whose boys were great horse riders, and after that it was farmed by Mr Chalk. Then a blind gentleman, Mr Howells, took it over and farmed rabbits there. According to Mr and Mrs Bartlam his wife used to stand behind him on the tractor tapping his shoulders, right and left depending in which direction they needed to go! This then became a general and dairy farm run by the Garrett family who arrived in Braishfield in the 1960s. Eric Irish worked there when it was dairy and arable. Finally Mr and Mrs Garrett's sons took over. They had a fine pedigree dairy herd which, sadly, they had to sell in the spring of 2000.

Eric Irish (right) and Norman Pitman unloading mangels from a cart at Fairbournes Farm in the mid-1950s.

Right: Corn being threshed in 1983 in the field at Woolley Green Farm called Lower Chestleys. Butler family members who returned each year to help in the harvest camped in the fields. The field is believed to be the site of several habitations going back seven thousand years and also the site of the Battle of Pucknall when Alfred defeated the Danes in 806; the blood was supposed to have run down Jermyns Lane, where there is a bridge called Bloody Bridge.

Far right: Widgeon thatching wheat grown on the field called Upper Chestleys. Sheaves are 'stooked' by hand to enable them to dry out and cure. This is highly skilled work, as the stooks have to be constructed to form four triangles to resist wind and give them protection against rain. Corn has been grown on this field, which is believed to have been the site of a Roman farm, for centuries. Various remains, including a stone quorn used for grinding corn now in the British Museum, have been found here.

Fernhill Farm is now farmed by Peter and David Vine. It was a pig farm previously, owned by Mr Hayward. Roger Bartlam owns **The Homestead** in Braishfield Road. He kept pigs, rabbits and turkeys which was a popular source for buying our Christmas dinners. The smallholding is still run for horses by Rosemary and Roger who also supply animal feed.

Newport Inn Farm, originally farmed by Mr Cooper and Mr Madgwick, was eventually taken over by my father, Alec Cottle. His family farmed near Devizes but there was not enough land for all of the family to work so he came to work in Southampton as a commercial traveller. At the start of the Second World War he tried to serve with the navy however his knowledge of Southampton streets made him more useful as a fireman! It was because of one such fire, in a pub owned by the Cottles' landlord, that the Cottles were invited to live in Braishfield.

The war effort here was in full swing. People collected their pigswill from a common source sent down from Middlesex. This swill was quite 'up-market' as it even contained

The Newport Inn in 1952.

54

The Cottle family at the door of the Newport Inn in 1951. Alec and Elsie with Janet, Shirley and Edna (kneeling).

silverware from some of London's best hotels! Over the age of ten, the children were allowed to go 'spud-bashing', then later in the summer to go gleaning the fields for corn. The kids on the spud bashing trips were very naughty and used to throw the potatoes at each other, making the farm workers cross. The farm workers included the Women's Land Army which is how Joan Parsons arrived in the village. The children also latched on to the farm carts, quickly collecting any mangels, kale or turnips if they fell off for use at home.

The Newport itself was a typical farm pub. In those days farming rather

Two corn ricks awaiting threshing in 1983 in Roman Field at Woolley Green. Most corn was stored in dutch barns at the farmstead but this was a good harvest, and storage room was short, so these ricks were put up. The Victorian system was to rick the corn in the fields until the winter and then to thresh it out by a contractor.

Alec and Elsie Cottle behind the bar at the Newport Inn in March 1965.

than the beer earned most money. The Dog and Crook, too, used to sell pigs as a sideline. Another source of income came from all the Americans stationed nearby at Hursley. In times of rationing the GIs were keen to barter. Parachute silk was useful for the dressmakers. Our water was pumped by an electric pump from a well … pure well water. When eventually mains water was connected the pressure burst the pipes which were all corroded.

Janet Cook is landlady of the famous Newport Inn. Her memories begin with the move to Braishfield with her sisters, Shirley and Edna, in 1941. Their parents, Alec and Elsie Cottle, took over the Newport Inn as tenants. Janet won a scholarship to Southampton Girls' Grammar School. During the war the school was moved to Bournemouth and Janet commuted daily by bus and train. Following school, like other girls from Braishfield, she worked at Hursley with Vickers-Armstrong, then later at IBM. Janet was a founder member of the Braishfield Seven Concert Party. She married Bernard Cook in 1969 and since then their life has centred on The Newport which is renowned for the Saturday night sing-songs with Janet at the piano. She began the tradition of an annual party for the older village residents.

TAP ROOM

Farming

1929–1989

Top:
One of Mr Owen's heifers, 'Braishfield Countess 2nd', held by Reg Randall in the paddock at Elm Grove in 1929. Mr Owen's prize-winning cattle were shown regularly and whereas the heifers were kept for breeding the selected bull was fattened for the Christmas fat stock show at Salisbury. It was taken for a walk round the lanes each day to harden off its feet. Before the show it was washed in Fairy Snow and groomed; after the show it was slaughtered by one of the local butchers, either Stares or Webbs, and the Owens and all the farm workers had a share of the meat.

Bottom:
A horse drawn binder at Elm Grove in the early 1940s. Reg Randall is on the extreme left.

Top left:
Jess Wells harvesting at Elm Grove in the late 1940s.

Top right:
Tea break at harvest time on 28th August 1954. Left to right: Sonner Old, ? Frank Matthews, George Fielder, Alec Cottle, Percy Cudmore.

Fairbournes Farm in 1947; laying the yard and drive from the house to Kiln Lane down to concrete. It was all mixed and laid by hand. The yard had been made of earth and flint and became very muddy when wet. This was the first major job Mr Cook undertook after taking over the farm. The building behind Mr Cook on the left was the last brick kiln in the village and was pulled down in the late 1950s. There were two brick kilns on Fairbournes Farm, the second being half way up Kiln Lane. Left to right: Felix Cook, Eric Irish, Jim Dunford, Freddie Hatton.

Norman Pitman in the mid-1950s standing up bales at Fairbournes Farm in a field off Kiln Lane.

A tractor and binder in the field above Newport House in 1959. Reg Randall is driving with his son, Peter, riding on the back of the binder. The windmill in the background drove a water pump.

Pucknall Farm in June 1985; Rusty Smith with tractor and plough.

Loading sheaves for threshing onto a trailer at Woolley Green Farm in 1989. Three trailers keep the threshing outfit going, yielding six tonnes of grain and nine hundred bundles of straw. Very few farms produce this straw largely because of the high cost of labour, risk from bad weather and high expertise needed. The variety of wheat is called widgeon, grown specially for its long straw suitable for thatching; it yields a high protein wheat for bread. It is labour intensive but Woolley Green has its own equipment and uses family labour. The work is physically hard especially in hot weather. Thatching straw has to be grown to a severe standard, the crop over forty inches long and, as the stem is brittle, it needs to be handled like bone china. Most of the houses in Kings Somborne are thatched with straw from this farm. This crop is used in rotation after grass grazed with sheep.

The Carpenter's Daughter
Alma Fail

1920s–1940s

My great grandfather, John Travis, lived at 2 Newport Lane. He was the village carpenter and undertaker. My father, Henry Travis, took over from his grandfather John. His workshop was situated just beyond The Lichens, on the plot where Mr and Mrs Eustace's house, Rupert Cottage, stands. I remember when they pitched the coffins it made a dreadful smell. Opposite was a chapel, afterwards used by the Boy Scouts. After lying empty for some years it was bought by Ken Foreman in the 1950s and he set it up as an engineering workshop. There was a shed on the other side of The Lichens, next to the Lipsett's house, where Bobby Lipsett's father would mend bikes in the late 1920s and early 1930s.

Alma Fail as a child in 1925 in front of the War Memorial. The farm buildings in the background were part of George Saunders' yard.

Going on down Newport Lane, just beyond the chapel on the right, was a pair of thatched cottages where Folly's End now stands.

The Braishfield School netball teams in 1934. Alma is in the front row on the left. Left to right: Back row: ?, Joan Archer, Joan Pinhorn, Dorrie Fielding, Ena Dewey, Margaret Old, Betty Thorne. Front row: Alma Travis, Maggie Moody, Peggy Cawte, ?, Doris Dewey, ?, Joy Logan.

Braishfield Road looking north from the end of Newport Lane, taken before 1902 when the clock tower was added to All Saints' Church.

A Mr Bennett lived there in the 1920s and he was the first one in Braishfield to have a motor car. The cottages had their gardens on the opposite side of the lane.

My grandfather, Harry Travis, was estate carpenter for Mr King of Braishfield Manor. He lived in Bowling Green Cottage, now Necton Cottage, in Paynes Hay Lane. When Mr Cobbold came from Essex as blacksmith he lodged with my grandparents and then Mr King built Bowling Green Bungalow for him when he married. Behind my grandparents' house was the forge and then beyond that the carpenter's workshops where the Oldens live in the house called The Old Forge.

I was born at 1 The Gardens. There were three pairs of cottages in The Gardens then. My mother's parents

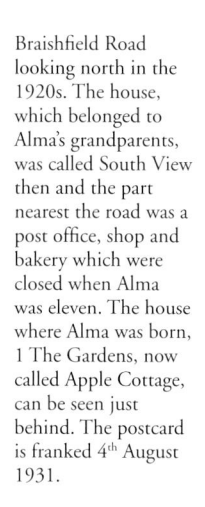

Braishfield Road looking north in the 1920s. The house, which belonged to Alma's grandparents, was called South View then and the part nearest the road was a post office, shop and bakery which were closed when Alma was eleven. The house where Alma was born, 1 The Gardens, now called Apple Cottage, can be seen just behind. The postcard is franked 4th August 1931.

Cottages at Pitt Farm under construction by builders including Henry Travis, the village carpenter, in the white apron. 'Knocker' Pottle is on Henry Travis' left.

were Fielders who lived up at Farley but originally came from Hursley way. They ran a post office, stores and bakery at South View, now called Swallowfield. They were no relation of the Fielders of Lower Street, who also had a bakery. My cousin Ida lived at 6 The Gardens. Her father was in the First World War and he died of his wounds afterwards. Rita Stitt and Girlie Old got his name, W Clelford, added to the War Memorial. My grandmother was very, very strict. Once, on the morning of the chapel outing, she wouldn't let my mother go until she had scrubbed the kitchen table, so the charabanc had to wait!

My grandad's brother lived in The Square where Mr and Mrs Musselwhite live. With Aunt Edith and Uncle Henry Fielder lodged a man named Bill Bailey. He had a room on the end of the house, which was a cobbler's shop, so we could have our boots and shoes repaired.

My first married home was at Number 1, The Terrace in Newport Lane. There was a communal tap for the six houses. After my husband came home from the war we moved to 7 Common Hill. Mr Betteridge had the shop opposite the school. When we heard that oranges had come in, my neighbour would ask me to get some for both of us. I would run down to the shop but Mr Betteridge would say, "Tell Mrs Webb, if it's not worth coming, they're not worth having!"

We had a taxi service, in Dores Lane, at what is now Pucknall House. With Mr and Mrs Williams lived her brother Jettie Goulding who was the owner of the taxi – a little cheaper than now.

Alma at South View, now Swallowfield, the original village post office. The flag celebrates the Coronation of King George VI in 1937.

Mrs King held wonderful Christmas parties at the Manor for the children. When I was a girl it was a great excitement going up there. We all joined the Band of Mercy and we had to recite, "I promise to be kind to all animals and to do all in my power to stop them from ill-usage".

Alma Fail (born Alma Travis) has lived in Braishfield all her life. After attending Braishfield School she went into service with Dr and Mrs Johnson at Linden House, Romsey. She returned home to look after her mother, married Ted Fail and brought up her family. Employed at Reed and Mallick for twenty-six years she then became the caretaker of Braishfield School. Now in her early eighties, she has lived in Common Hill for just over fifty years and shares her home with her daughter Janet Blake, who is the present school caretaker!

The Blacksmith's Daughter
Patricia Foxcroft

1932–1956

I was the daughter of Albert Cobbold, the village blacksmith, born in 1932 in the same year as Mum and Dad bought Bowling Green Bungalow and the accompanying forge and workshop from the Braishfield Manor Estate. I was born in the bungalow. Both Bowling Green Bungalow and the forge were demolished some years ago and other properties built in their place. Where the forge stood is now a house called The Old Forge. In the place of the bungalow is a newly built chalet bungalow.

Paynes Hay Lane is a typical Hampshire agricultural setting bordered as it is the whole length by farmers' cornfields and few dwellings, but which does include Braishfield Manor and Paynes Hay Farm. When we had heavy rain the lane used to flood a good deal. I learnt later that the lane followed what was in earlier years the bottom of a riverbed and the rainwater was slow to drain away or dry up because of that. The main part of the village lies about three-quarters of a mile distant from where we lived. We used to knock off a quarter of that by taking the footpath which passed by the bottom of our garden and linked Paynes Hay Lane with the lane from Farley into Braishfield.

Captain Sir John Alleyne (left) presenting a shield to Mr Albert Cobbold at the Young Farmers' Club Rally at Broadlands in May 1969. John King is mounted and Sally Rawson-Smith is on the right.

I was an only child, just seven years old when the 1939–45 World War started and twelve when it ended. Dad was not conscripted during the war because his trade was agricultural and so exempted him. As I grew up I came to realise that he was a true country person and so was I.

During the war and for some years after horse shoeing slackened off to almost non-existent. It was then that Dad learnt spot welding and iron fusing which he put to good use repairing any and every kind of agricultural equipment that the farmers brought into him. New equipment then was not to be had.

65

The yard at Paynes Hay Farm in 1935 when it was owned by General Cuthbertson. Harry Mason, pictured, was the carter then. General Cuthbertson was the first farmer in the village to have inflatable tyres on carts, metal gates to fields and metal holding pens. The Cobbold's property bordered Paynes Hay Farm.

I suppose really my earliest memories of life in the village revolve around the 'Blacksmith Shop' as we and the local folk always called it. Built of wood and covered with a galvanised roof, the shop was set in a half acre of ground with entrance and exit by Paynes Hay Lane and a field of Willett's Farm bordering the other side. This field could only be reached by crossing my Dad's ground. Like so many village arrangements of those days it was settled by gentlemen's agreement made between my Dad and the farmer that he could use an out of the way crossing across the ground. This agreement existed to my knowledge without animosity for some forty years.

Inside the shop was the blacksmith's forge with huge bellows and ventilator flue, a blacksmith's anvil, a bench, drilling tools and other paraphernalia. I can visualise now the sooty and smoke-blackened walls and see Dad with smutty face and glistening leather work apron, poised over anvil, with hammer in right hand and tongs holding a red-hot glowing piece of steel in the other. To me as a little girl a visit to my Dad's shop was always fascinating; to see him shoeing a great big hunter horse and doing it with a red-hot shoe from which smoke billowed, for instance. All the time he had to avoid that huge weight of horse treading on his feet.

Dad used to work very long hours always being available to shoe a horse 'hot' at his shop or go to a client within his area range to 'cold' shoe a horse – regular customers of course were our bread and butter. Goodness knows how he could identify which shoe amongst old ones came off a horse he had shod before because there seemed to be old shoes littering or hung up

The cross roads by Braishfield Manor looking east up Farley Lane towards Farley Chamberlayne. Manor Cottage is just visible on the right, with Pitt Farm in the trees on the left. The sign post is marked 'Braishfield & Romsey' to the right, 'Kings Somborne & Stockbridge' to the left.

everywhere in the shop. It wasn't often Mum and I were allowed to tidy up the shop for fear of Dad saying, "I can't find anything when I want it now." The work carried on ticking over anyhow.

I cannot remember any time that we did not keep three or four dozen chickens and cockerels up the shop and some years we also kept a pig or two. Mum used to prepare chickens and cockerels for the oven and always had ready buyers from local folk and others.

Periodical visitors to see my father were from the Romany encampments at Kings Somborne. The 'Barneys', as we knew them, used to come and buy scrap iron and other stuff from my Dad. They were always friendly and, whatever deals were made, seemingly fair. As Dad used to say, "Treat them fairly and they will do the same for you" – and I believe it was so.

Another character I vividly remember was Mr Boxer Old. He used to own a combine harvester and a vintage steam engine with which he used to undertake any kind of suitable agricultural work such as harvesting, fence making and log cutting. Mr Old used to garage them on a piece of adjoining land to my Dad's.

Interesting and true; Dad was also considered the village barber. He had bought a barber's set of clippers, etc., and the shop was an old packing case at his workshop. He used to charge ninepence for a short back and sides. The proceeds from this venture were given to me as my pocket money.

A means of transport was required, of course, and after a bicycle in the early days, a succession of second hand cars to carry his tools and self around the area were purchased. I remember his first car was an Austin Seven, then a Singer, followed by a van of sorts, and then best of all of them, a Morris Traveller 1000. Needless to say they carried some rough and weighty stuff, but a family trip out in them was always a treat.

I attended Braishfield Village School for the whole of my schooling. The teachers at that time were Mrs Dane, headmistress, also Mrs Benham and Miss Penfold. At twelve years the girls would go to one of the schools in Romsey for a once a week cookery lesson. The big laugh amongst us children was to see the cookery teacher, Miss Plumer, riding upon her 'sit up and beg' bicycle with its special guards over the large wheels to protect her long frocks from going into the wheel spokes.

At the age of fourteen I left school. Time had moved on from the peace and quiet of a country village to the wartime.

During the Battle of Britain Southampton suffered a great deal of bombing and we in Braishfield were the spectators of it. There were the huge, white and grey-bellied barrage balloons moored high above the dock areas. Sirens sounded night and day. Searchlights and explosions lit up the sky. One evening Dad and I happened to be on our way to our bungalow when, looking up, we saw an aeroplane on fire diving out of the sky. Dad picked me up and into the bungalow and under the dining room table we went.

Closer to home there was an army gun site located on Sauce Hill, near Braishfield House and a searchlight on Casbrook Common. The Home Guard had their headquarters at

Pat and Ray Foxcroft on the occasion of the christening of their son, Stephen in September 1957, together with Pat's parents, Albert and Ella Cobbold.

Joe and Arthur Cardy standing by a W Stares butcher's van in the 1930s,

General (Retired) Ransome's house, The Close, near to the church. Mum used to help clean the HQ offices as part of her war work. Besides that she and I used to help the landgirls collect potatoes from the farmers' fields.

During the war years entertainment was not readily available in the village for a young girl. We did have the village hall, which was also the Women's Institute, and three pubs, The Newport, Dog and Crook and the Wheatsheaf, of course. Occasionally a dance would be organised at the village hall and the soldiers from the gun site would come along, particularly as it was their band that supplied the music. In the main however our main source of entertainment, I guess, was the radio. Who of my generation and the one before will ever forget Charlie Chester and Itma. Another memorable occasion was the excitement caused when a German bomb landed in the village allotments. Fortunately it failed to explode and in due course was removed by the soldiers.

Always we had to carry about with us our gas masks, which were contained in a cardboard box and slung from one's shoulder by a cord strap. I only ever put it on my face and head once and that was when I was first issued with it. It never did happen that 'Jerry' dropped gas on us, but the threat to us that it might happen was ever real, I assure you.

Before, during and after the war we always had a milkman, baker, butcher and grocer regularly call and deliver to us. The coal man and oil man – important fuel for heating and cooking – always used to deliver orders, too.

Pat receiving a prayer book from the Rector, Samuel Boothman, in November 1955 when she resigned as organist before leaving to join her husband in Malaya. The four senior members of the choir in the back represent well over one hundred and fifty years service between them. Left to right: Back row: Albert Cobbold, George Parsons, Samuel Boothman, Sidney Scorey, Pat, Derek Elkins, Fred Abraham (in profile). Front row: Wendy Eastwood, John Hance, Jean Benham, Colin Beeson, Elizabeth Benham.

Getting to and from Romsey was no problem for Mum and I. We 'got on our bikes'. I really cannot remember what and whether any public transport was available because people did not travel far during the war. Mum used to like to use the Co-operative Stores in Romsey and they would always deliver.

On Sundays before the war there was always the 'Stop me and buy one' ice cream tricycle passing down Paynes Hay Lane and I was always there waiting with my Dad. I missed that treat during the war.

At fourteen I became the regular church organist and continued playing until 1956. Our organ then was air operated and had to be pumped by a lever located at the back of the organ. This duty was performed by Charlie Saunders. Regrettably I cannot tell you the history of this organ. I was married in All Saints', Braishfield, in 1954 and the reception was held in the old village hall-cum-Women's Institute. My husband was a soldier and soon after our wedding he was sent to join the British Commonwealth Division in Korea and Japan. I stayed in Braishfield until I could rejoin him eighteen months later in Malaya.

Coming back to Braishfield to see my parents and friends was always a delight to me. Both my children, Stephen and Hilary, were baptized in All Saints' by the same rector who married me, Canon Samuel Boothman.

I used to notice the many changes happening in the village: a new village hall to replace the old one, now a house called Bryndlewood

Pat with her father in Paynes Hay Lane.

stands in its place. The Old Village Store, and off-licence from the wartime, is still there but used for living accommodation only. Many large properties have since sprung up all over the village.

My parents are buried at All Saints' and the church notice board was erected to their memory.

Albert Cobbold began his life with horses as a groom at a stud near Bury St Edmunds moving to Braishfield to take the position of groom, farrier and general smith with Mrs King at Braishfield Manor where he worked at her hackney pony stud until it was sold in 1933. He bought the estate forge and the bungalow in Paynes Hay Lane and set up on his own account, forging all his own shoes and carrying out welding and farm machinery repairs within a radius of about twenty miles.

In 1967 he was awarded a plaque at the Royal International Horse Show at White City in London as top farrier in the hunter classes.

Though he always retained his Suffolk accent, his 'Suffolk song', he was very much a man of Braishfield and played an active role in the community as both parish and church councillor, school governor, church choir member and chairman of the Braishfield Social Club. When he retired in 1975 the equestrian and agricultural community honoured his forty years' service with a presentation in recognition of his life's work. He died in 1982 aged seventy-nine.

Pat and her husband, Ray, travelled far and wide in the course of Ray's career in the RAF. When he retired they settled in Salisbury near their children Stephen and Hilary.

From a Countryman's Diary
Norman Goodland

1947–1960s

Fifty years ago and more we came to live in Eldon Lane which runs from Kings Somborne to Braishfield, a memory lane now for us when we motor past the farm, Hall Place, where I was once dairyman, and the farm cottage where we lived, which was part of Greenacres. We remember the postman who lived next door and the spiderman in the cottage below who worked on the pylons then being erected across the countryside. Past Highfield where between milkings my wife and I sometimes joined the hoeing gang and, pausing to stretch our backs, we could see on a clear day the smoke from the steamships as they rounded the corner of a grey and far distant Isle of Wight.

I've kept diaries on and off all my life and many of my Radio Solent talks have been culled from them.

The Dairyman

A piece from my diary, 20th January 1947, when I was a dairyman then at Malthouse Farm in the Parish of Braishfield.

At six o'clock I light my paraffin lamp and wake my wife. She bemoans the hard lot of the dairyman's wife. Well she might. For when we're finished milking, she'll be out there,

Hall Place Cottage, now Greenacres, where Norman and Sylvia lived. Robin Sheppard, who bought Hall Place Farm in 1962, is ploughing the field on the opposite side of Eldon Lane.

in the cold, washing up the dairy things, washing down the cowpen. A swift cup of tea for us both, then off I go in my rough clothes and rough coat, cloth-capped and unshaven, across to the farm. Hundreds of leaden mirrors, water-filled castes of cow's hooves, deep set in mud, reflect a rainy dawn. I search for the dung-prong to prop open the half doors against the wind.

Two heifers, recently arrived, lie in at nights because the boss wasn't sure whether they were hardened to the winter or not. They lie idly in their bays; long red legs stretched comfortably across the litter. The roan in the loose box is up, eyeing me with huge liquid eyes, letting me know her trough is empty. Her calf in the corner still sleeps. In the bay at the further end two two-month old calves rustle straw and vie with each other bleating for milk.

I feed round the empty mangers with brewers' grains, crushed oats and hay. I'm being just a bit quiet about it, for a good reason. Out again in the semi-darkness I slop through the mud to open the five-barred gate leading into Home Field. Dim, silent shapes stand patiently on the other side.

My shoulder brushes the hen-run. A wire netting hand bobs forward to scatter ice-cold drops upon my face. I drop the gate off its hook, smoothing out a half circle of mud with the bottom bar as I push it open. In come the cows with huge rough legs and knock knees, sailing their hulks through the mud, one behind the other. And in they go with swinging horns and tails, each to its own stall.

Woe betide me if, half asleep and not thinking, I ever forget to feed round the mangers first. For then big Milly will give one disgusted snort; our

Most dairy herds in the village were Friesian. While Norman and Sylvia milked at Malthouse, here Premier, from the Fairbournes herd, comes to get titbits over the garden hedge from Jean Irish.

long-legged roan kicker, Nancy, will do the same, and they'll try to move off out again, pushing and shoving against the others still trying to come in.

But this morning all is well. I move among them, chaining them up, fixing the rings over the T-pieces to prevent chains working undone, making sure the swivels run free to prevent throttling. And I'm as quiet as possible about that, too. Next, water from the dairy, a touch of disinfectant, and quick washing of udders. They are all plastered in mud which slows me down.

And then the old upright Petter engine that creates the vacuum for milking starts up in the engine shed! Damn! The boss has got there first! You see, after the cows are tied up and washed, whoever gets to the engine first can claim the other one's late! And the penalty for that is to milk Nancy, the roan kicker!

But there's still another ploy. If I can grab the milking buckets from the dairy first **I** can choose where to start milking! No chance! The boss comes in, all smiles, a bucket and cups in each hand. He puts one set down for me and starts at the far end. Which means I have to start this end, so I come to Nancy first.

Ah, well, there's always another day! Can't win 'em all, can you?

Going for Daffodils

Off to the daffodil farm beyond Winchester to get a sackfull of flowered bulbs. If you do that you heel them in, and plant them out again in September, and just wait to see what varieties you have in the following spring. It can be quite exciting. At our horticultural society's spring show, the judge brought in specimen blooms. Of one he said you might have to pay five pounds for a single bulb – and we realized that we'd got some already!

We passed through Winchester City going and coming back, and have done for years, to avoid its by-pass. Sounds ridiculous really, but a lot of us locals prefer that, because even on the one-way routes around the city conservation areas there is still so much of the old, the familiar – the ancient – to see. And little shops, and stores – just as there were when we were young, and coming back we've always found it easy enough.

Back over downland – so wide, so free, with great trees – especially the beeches – just about at bud-breaking in the dips and the hollows and the vales. At Standon we decided to turn

The road past Woolley Green looking towards Lower Slackstead and the road to Winchester.

away from the traffic and go up into that network of winding, downland lanes at the back of home. We wound on up the hill with copseland at its very top still managed in the old way, and the bluebells rank-on-rank in the sparse springtime shade, a vast multitude of royal blue. On past the seemingly endless ancient stone wall of the old Hursley Estate. Wind, wind, wind – and I'm reminded again of an old ballad Peter Dawson used to sing – I've still got it somewhere on an old 78 – something about the rollicking English drunkard who built the winding English lanes.

You **could** think so but you know wherever there's a bend there was once something there to make you go round. I wondered again what these might have been; great old fallen trees, dense woodlands, bog-pockets, properties, perhaps dwellings of long ago. Original foot tracks probably, then cart, or waggon, or pony-and-trap, or perhaps they were merely the most level stretches between the feet of the downs. But today nobody but the birds, the rabbits or the deer are living here; no development, no strategic route from here to there, only the occasional car or van or farm tractor to be met or to pull in for – or they for you; whoever comes this way **can't** be in a hurry. Until you get into the outlying hamlets where farmer, or indigenous cottager, or monied newcomer having turned his purchase into yet another mini-mansion, glances at or ignores the intruder – which, of course, you are.

On down to the villages where you are not. Old Farmer Black's long black farmhouse still commands the hill against the sky and ahead, stepping out from Pucknall Farm gate with head high and fearless stare, a tall peahen is followed by three even taller swains holding heavy, incredibly long, multi-coloured tails just

75

John Bethal and Bill Gregory at the Newport Inn in 1948.

clear of the ground – expecting us to slow right down, which we did – to let them leisurely cross. Where else but on an English lane built by Peter Dawson's rollicking drunkard would you see that?

On to the fork in the road taking the right, down past the church to the War Memorial showing the names of the men of Braishfield who fell in two world wars, names known only to generations of the indigenous – but now meaning less and less to passers-by. And then down to the Newport – mine hosts Janet and Bernard Cook. When my wife and I came to work as dairywoman and dairyman in Braishfield and were newly moved in to Malthouse Farm Cottage, we took a break from decorating at the Newport, spattered with whitewash. We're still reminded of it from time to time. Miraculously, it has hardly changed from those times with the result that everybody, town or country, knows it and its weekends are packed – with Janet at the piano.

This was the pub where Bernard was ticked off by the Health Man for having a spider's web in the corner of the toilet. Bernard told him he kept a trained spider up there to keep down the flies so that they didn't come through to the bar.

As we ordered there was a burst of hammering on the cellar ceiling beneath our feet. Janet said without batting an eyelid, "Woodworm!" But Bernard said, "The Health Man again. We're boarding the cellar ceiling so the dust and the germs don't fall in the beer when you walk about!" "But", I said, "The beer's in cask and you pump straight up from it!" "Well!" reflected Bernard, "You know that – I know that – and so do the

Peter Gritt in 1959 driving a tractor with seed drill at Malthouse Farm where Norman learned to plough. Norman is on the drill.

germs. But these days we got to do as we're told by those above us – here and in Brussels – who get paid a lot of our money – for knowing jugger-all!"

And so home. I can just about heave-down the **two** sacks of daffodils – not one! And my wife, rejuvenated by a vision of springtime gold, leaves me spade-in-hand, puzzled about heeling-in where she hasn't planted already!

Norman is Hampshire born and bred. He and his wife, Sylvia, came to Braishfield in the 1940s as dairyman and dairywoman to Leslie Harris at Malthouse Farm, living in a cottage behind the farmhouse. He later worked for Leslie's brother, George, at Hall Place. A writer and poet, he started broadcasting with the BBC in the 1960s, giving talks on farming and the countryside. He has written books about rural life in Hampshire's bygone days and continues to broadcast his Hampshire stories on BBC Radio Solent. He and his wife now live in Timsbury.

Elm Grove Childhood
Dilys Grieve (1906–2001)

1906–1930s

Left: Dilys Grieve in September 1983 with her Pembrokeshire corgi, Cariad.

Right: W G Owen of Elm Grove Farm in the late 1930s.

Miss Janet Eaton of Braishfield House tending a pig.

Coming across an old guide book of Hampshire I found that Braishfield was described as a 'remote hamlet'. The arrival of the motorcar and electricity has changed the remoteness of all country villages and mechanical agricultural implements have reduced to a great extent the number of people working on the land. In some ways this is a loss as the country people then were so interested in the land and the animals that working by the clock was not important.

Braishfield House belonged to a Miss Janet Eaton who also owned Elm Grove Farm. She was a great character and given to much hospitality, but unfortunately the lovely old Georgian house was burnt down and the lady reduced to camping under the cedar tree on the lawn until it was rebuilt as a bungalow on the old foundations. This, in its turn, was subjected to the same fiery fate when Mr Newby Vincent lived there and he then built the present house, also on the same site.

Elm Grove Farm in the 1920s with Mr W G Owen's prize-winning herd of pedigree dairy shorthorns.

Braishfield Manor was bought by Mr Alfred Charles King who also purchased Pitt Farm, Paynes Hay Farm, Hall Farm and Malthouse Farm. His manager, who ran all these farms, was my father, Mr William G Owen, affectionately known in the neighbourhood as WG. He lived at Elm Grove Farm from about 1904 until he died at the age of 76.

Mrs King kept a stud of Hackney ponies at Paynes Hay Farm and a pleasant sight they were, each looking out of their stables, also to be seen in training on the roads and being driven in tandem in light gigs. The stud stallion's name was Harveston Wattie and he is commemorated on a weather vane which can still be seen on the Manor stable roof but which I'm sure is now occupied by a horseless carriage.

A herd of Dexter cattle was kept at Paynes Hay Farm and cream churned into lovely butter there.

WG, who bought Elm Grove later on the death of Mr King, bred a prize-winning herd of pedigree dairy shorthorns with the prefix 'Braishfield'. They won many prizes at local and national shows, and some more recently were exported.

Braishfield Lodge was bought by Admiral Sir Reginald Bacon who lived there during the years of his retirement. He was in charge of the Home Guard during the war.

Aerial view of Elm Grove Farm in the early 1960s.

Elm Grove on a Sunday afternoon in the early 1950s. On the left is Reg Randall with his son, Peter, aged six, and Roy Willis.

Fortunately no real damage was done to the village but one bomb fell on Elm Grove in the lower pasture field and the crater it left can still be seen.

I remember during one severe thunderstorm the church tower was struck and needed extensive repairs. Also during another storm much later a meteor fell in the road near the school. It was about the size of a tennis ball and heavy and of dull brass.

One of the highlights of the agricultural year was the harvest supper which Mr and Mrs King gave for all their employees in a building behind the Manor. WG always presided and took me along in case an accompaniment should be needed on the piano during the impromptu entertainment which followed the enjoyable supper – but none ever was. Mrs White sang 'Little Brown Jug', Mr White 'We shall meet her at the ball tonight boys' and Joe Holbrook obliged with 'The fly be on the turnip' and many others, all great fun. Port wine and plum cake and a sing-song ended a happy evening.

I remember our carter, Mr Savage, who would rise at five in the morning to get the pair of shire horses ready in the wagon and all the brasses sparkling to drive to Romsey Station to collect a load of cattle cake from the train. It was a wonderful turnout and won many prizes at Romsey Show.

One Sunday evening our parents had gone to church when there was suddenly a terrific mooing of cattle and confusion in the cow pens. So, plucking up courage, my sister and I went out to find Sam Munday, the dairyman, tying the cows in their stalls without much success. When I asked him what he was doing he said, "Milkin' ", surprised at my question. When I told him they had been milked I pointed to the setting sun. He said, "Good heavens, I be somewheres today." Apparently he had taken too much beer earlier and fell asleep in the lane on his way back to his cottage at Fernhill. On waking he thought it was early morning and was, as he thought, making up for his Sunday afternoon lapse by being very early Monday morning! He came in for much teasing when it became known in the village.

Remembered, too, with affection were the Abraham family who kept the village shop with a bakehouse in which they baked the bread in an old-fashioned oven heated by faggots of wood burnt in it which were then drawn out and the loaves put in. The bread was delicious, especially the crusty cottage loaf. Wood for this was cut by them from Parnholt Wood and stacked in huge piles ready for use. The bakehouse is no longer there but the shop survives. Miss Gertrude Abraham had never been as far as Southampton until my sister drove her there in the car about the late 1920s. She sold beer at the shop and always referred to it as ale.

Another family I remember were the Pottles who lived in a long thatched cottage by the Elm Grove gate. They ran a carrier service to Winchester and brought shopping back for the village people who had no means of getting there themselves. Eli Pottle lived there after the business was given up and remained there until he died. By that time the cottage was in rather a bad state so had to be demolished, sadly, and a small bungalow built in its place.

A flock of sheep were kept at Pitt Farm and every lambing time a lovely fold was erected in Taunton Vale sheltered from the winds by sheep

Elm Grove horses and cart in the 1930s at the Romsey Show. The driver is Ernest Savage, the head carter.

WG Owen with his horse, Betty Wynne.

hurdles and faced with straw, one cubicle for each ewe. The shepherd, Edgar Rogers, lived there also at this time in his caravan.

WG used to ride his favourite horse, Betty Wynne, who he always described as a weight-carrying cob, around all the farms and saw every man wherever he was working, most mornings leaving the house at eight o'clock in the morning and seldom returning before eleven-thirty.

This memory is believed to have been written in the 1970s and was held in safekeeping by the WI.

Mr and Mrs Pottle and daughter, Amy, outside Elm Grove Farm Cottage in the early 1920s. Mr Pottle had his own business as a carrier, sometimes known as 'Pottle's Pony'. The cottage was in Dummers Road between the pond and the farm gate. A chalk and flint cottage, it was demolished in the first year of the war and replaced by the present brick-built bungalow.

Dilys was born at Elm Grove and lived there with her parents, William Gladstone (WG) and Mary Owen, and her younger sister, Betty, until her marriage to Michael Grieve, the son of a prominent Congregationalist. Betty married John Hoddinott and they farmed at Elm Grove after Mr Owen's death in 1952. After the war the Grieves returned from government service in Kenya to live in Braishfield at Spinney Corner. Dilys loved music and was an accomplished pianist. She died at Cerne Abbas in 2001.

People

1909–1960

The Old family at Pitt Farm between 1909 and 1911. Left to right: Back row: May Old, Kate Dummer, Walt Old holding Reg (Boxer), ?, Bob Old. Front row: probably Arthur Old (boy with cat), Nelly Old (nee Dummer – George Old's wife), ? Jim Old, Granny Dummer, Bertha Old (nee Dummer – Walt's wife). Granny Dummer's two daughters both married Old brothers.

David Marsh Thorne and his family in the mid-1920s outside the school and opposite their shop in Common Hill Road. Rose Thorne is in the back with her son, Denzil, and Josephine is in the front with her father. There were few cars in the village then, according to Rosemary Mason, Mr Thorne's granddaughter: the Kings at the Manor; the Bacons at Braishfield Lodge; Mr Dummer who had the post office at the corner of Newport Lane; Mr Travis, the carpenter and undertaker; Jet Goulding's taxi; Tom Parsons, the dispenser for Dr Johnson in Romsey; Jim Parsons at Malthouse; and the Butlers at Hall Farm.

John Mason, the two landgirls Jean and Muriel, and an Italian prisoner of war, Santemarello, on a dung cart at Hall Farm in 1942. John used to walk with two prisoners of war along Eldon Lane to Kings Somborne and back to see a picture show which the Americans put on at Kings Somborne Village Hall. When asked if John was frightened, he replied, "No, I can run much faster than those two." The prisoners of war were based at Ganger Camp.

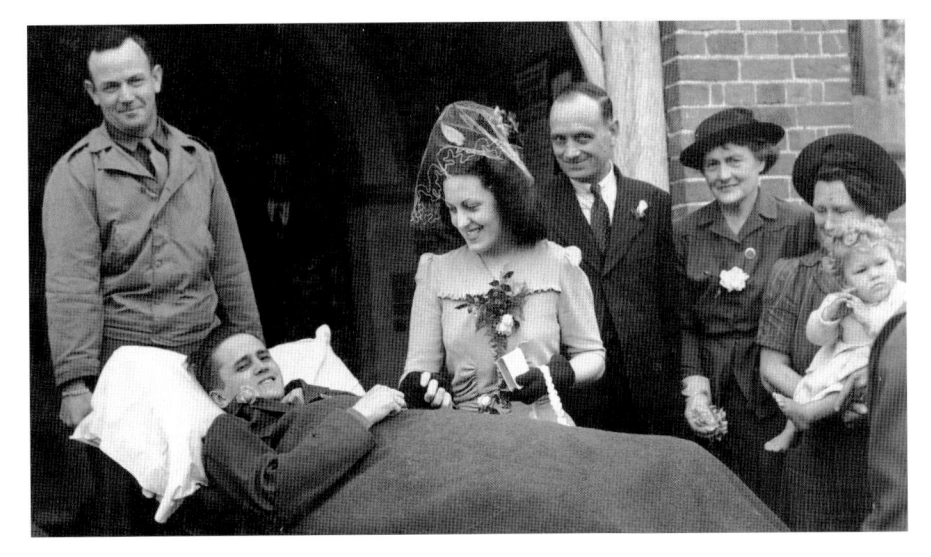

The wedding of Rita Old to Malcolm Stitt, an American GI, on 14th June 1945 at All Saints' Church. With Rita are her parents, Percival and Laura, and her sister Lily holding her daughter, Catherine. Malcolm's best man (left) was Corporal Benjamin Ruvolo.

A coach trip to Weymouth in the mid-1950s taken at Weymouth Bus Station. Mervyn Fielder is on the left with two farm workers from the Bossington Estate. Mervyn was working at Pitt Farm for Richard Willett whose uncle, Mr Bright, had Bossington Farm. The two farmers used to organise a coach trip to Weymouth between haymaking and harvest for their employees. Each man was given ten shillings, a week's wages, as he got off the bus. A boat was hired for those who wished to go mackerel fishing.

85

Members of the Social Club and competitors in the fancy dress competition at the club's annual fete taken by the south side of the old clubhouse in 1952 or 1953. The building stood opposite the chapel beside a disused sandpit, a site which was occupied subsequently by the Braishfield Garage and now the houses in Blackthorn Close. Left to right: Back row: ? (in hat), David Andrews, Norman Fielder, ?, ?, Mr Ross (chairman), Albert Cobbold, ?, Mrs Dunning of Merrie Mead, ?. Front row: including Jim Fail, Janet Fail, Doreen Fielding, Zena Simms (Queen of Hearts), John Burns (boxer), Norma White (cowgirl).

Dennis Harrington in 1959 or 1960 standing in front of Ken Foreman's steam traction engine outside the Newport Inn with the grounds of Battledene House (now Newport House) in the background. Mr Reg (Boxer) Old is on the engine and Bill Harrington, in the dark jacket, is one of the children standing on the cart.

A Schoolgirl in the Twenties
Clara Alice Hayter
as told to Ann Chant

1920–1930

When I was young we all lived in cottages near Fairbournes Farm. My parents were Tom and Clara Webb. My brother Tom and I were twins and I had another brother, Douglas, and a sister, May.

In those days there was no running water. Sometimes my brothers were sent to Mr Grace's for water. Once when Tom didn't come back I was sent to look for him. The bottle was overflowing on the ground and the pipe from the well still running. There was Tom over the road playing football. He'd forgotten about the water. Another time my mother sent me with a metal bucket. This was heavy for a little girl and I rested it down on the road while I watched the chickens and geese in the field. Along came Mr Wells, the butcher, riding on his cart. He didn't see the bucket, ran over and squashed it. I ran home in tears to tell my mother – a bucket was expensive – but my mum was kind saying, "Mr Wells, I'll give him bucket!"

Our front room was once a fish and chip shop and when Mr Grace came to clear the well he found it full of sea shells.

A man next door kept a donkey on a lead. We used to get water for it in a big pan. The donkey was used at threshing time and walked round and round working the machinery.

One evening mother went out to get paraffin and then we heard a loud thump. We were frightened. We all went out to have a look and half the house had fallen down – the end had gone! The landlord left it a few days and then put up a bit of corrugated iron. Sometime later the house was pulled down.

Once we were playing outside in the dark. We took off our coats and put them through the arm holes and

Clara and her twin brother, Tommy, in their guide and scout uniforms on their twelfth birthday, 27th July 1926.

Clara's father, Tom Webb. He worked as farmhand at Hall Farm, now Hall Place, in Eldon Lane and also as a thatcher before he joined the army. He was killed four days before Armistice was declared and was found lying across the body of his army captain. Both were killed by the same sniper.

ran about like that. Then we looked up and saw the sky was all red. My brother was frightened. Next day my mother said it was the 'Aurora Borealis'.

Miss Nutbeam and her brother farmed Fairbournes then. She used to keep a pig called Pinky and they used to walk to Braishfield Post Office together. Miss Nutbeam used to go about in a big bonnet with a frill around it. She was ever such a kind lady who used to let us play in the fields of the farm. Sometimes we would walk directly over the fields to Timsbury. We would pick kingcups for Miss Nutbeam.

Sometimes we would go out with the Goulding family next door. Mrs Goulding took in washing and her front was full of washing lines. One job we had was to fill a big old pram with clean washing and to push it to Woolley Lodge. The cook there would give us hot chocolate and biscuits. We liked her and didn't mind going if we had a treat at the end. Sometimes we took the cook a big bunch of primroses.

In later years another farmer, Mr Phillips from Wales, arrived at Lower Slackstead. He kept his young chickens and geese in incubators. On my way to buy eggs and milk from the farm I saw smoke coming from the sheds and the geese and chickens running about. I shooed some of them out of the way and went to tell the farmer. He came and shouted at me, "What are you doing?" Then he realised what was happening. Next time I went around to buy eggs and milk he said to tell my mum that we could have them free for the next month.

My brother Tom and I were in All Saints' Choir. At harvest time the church was beautifully decorated. We loved singing in the choir but I didn't like the dark and would run all the way home after choir practice on winter evenings.

My father's name is on the war memorial. He was killed on November the seventh. The Armistice was declared on the eleventh. We have a school photograph at about that time. Miss Euston taught us. She was a nice lady and a good teacher. Then Mrs Dane took over. She could be very strict. I had the cane on my hand every day of the week for being late. My mother had to go and help Miss Callendar and I was left to get my twin brother ready. He was so slow he made me late for school. Miss Dane said, "Hold out your hand" as soon as I got to school – so I got caned. Then I said to my brother, "You can lie in bed 'til dinner time, or all day, but I'm not going to be late."

Once when we needed wood we took a big axe up to Jermyn's Wood to the rhododendrons to get firewood. This time my mother was with us. The keeper arrived and asked, "What are you doing? Give me that axe!" Mother gave him the axe and then said, "I want my dad's axe back – you can keep the wood." In the end he gave us the wood and the axe.

At Christmas we went to parties at Braishfield Manor where Mrs King lived. Some people called her 'Lady King'. She would ride in a chariot (horse and open carriage) and when she passed we were supposed to bow or curtsy to her.

One Christmas at the Manor I was given a present and it was a golliwog. I had always wanted one and was thrilled to bits. I had had the golliwog for about four years when it went missing. We searched high and

Clara's class at Braishfield School in the early 1920s. Left to right: Back row: Miss Rhoda Euston from Ampfield, Clara Webb, Flossie or Doris Dewey, 'Ginger' Old, Raymond or Henry Dewey, Ivy Goulding, Tommy Webb, Virtue Davis (from the Wheatsheaf). Middle row: Ernie Miles, ?, ?, Fannie Holbrook, Lucy Randall, Charlie Swainston. Front row: Ivy Goodridge, Tom Webb (no relation to Clara and Tommy), ?, ?, ?, Jessie Coster, George Miles.

An embroidered card containing a handkerchief sent to Clara by her father from France. The message on the card reads, "To My Dear Little Sisie wishing her a very Happy Birthday and a lucky one. With Best Love and Kisses from Daddie for the 27th of July 1918. XXXXX."

low for him and eventually found him in a water butt. He was made of sawdust and was all swollen up. My brother Tom had put him there!

When I was older I got a job as a lady's maid to Lady Gurney-Dixon in The Close at Winchester. On my day off I cycled back to Braishfield but didn't like going back in the dark.

Clara was born in 1914. Her mother, born Clara Emily Barfoot, worked in the village for Miss Callendar. Her father, Tom Mitchel Webb, was a farmhand at Hall Place and also a thatcher.

After leaving school Clara became a lady's maid until the outbreak of the Second World War when she went to work at the Corporation Bus Depot in Southampton. She married Godfrey (Jim) Hayter in 1941 and has a son, John. She now lives in Romsey.

A Lifetime in One Place
Fannie Holbrook

1920–1930

A fancy dress party held on the lawn of Fairbournes Farm in 1929 for Tessa and Molly Philips, daughters of the farmer. Fannie Holbrook is dressed as a daffodil. Left to right: Back row: Vera Plummer, Gwennie Abraham (Mrs Holloway), Betty Old (Mrs Bill Pearce), Maggie Moody (Mrs Joe Newcombe), Jean Watts. Front row: Alma Travis (Mrs Ted Fail), Ida Clelford (Mrs Percy Chandler), Tessa Philips, Molly Philips, Joyce Old (Mrs George Alford), Fannie Holbrook, Margaret Old.

I was born at 3 Crook Cottages and have lived there for eighty-one years, the whole of my life.

I went to the council school and I remember the caretaker who used to clean the school was called Mr Nuddall. He used to stoke up the coal fires for us in all the rooms. The governess was Mrs Dane, and in my school days one teacher was called Miss Rogers and the other was Miss Euston. The school was divided into three classes; the first one was for the infants from five to six, the second one was from six onwards, and every year you would have an exam and those who got the highest points would go into Standard Four. They had that every year until you went right up into the governess' room where you got up to Standard Six.

When we were at school, we joined what they called the Band of Mercy and we had to say, "I promise to be kind to all animals and do all in my power to keep they from ill-usage". In those days Mrs King was in the big Manor house and she used to give us a nice Christmas tree when we went up there to the Manor, and a nice tea and we all had presents. We used to have to say our promise to her before we could start our meal.

Boring an artesian well. Fred Marsh, who worked for James Grace, is standing by a drilling rig. A metal windmill was erected to pump water for the immediate locality. Windmills were a common feature of the landscape until the late 1960s.

James Grace of Brook House had an artesian well-boring business and sank many of the wells in the village.

I was fourteen when I left Braishfield School and the governess, Mrs Dane, gave us a reference of what we were like to take with us when we got our first job.

I had a little time at home and then I went to work as a domestic for Mr and Mrs Dunning who were butchers in Southampton living up by the church. I was there for eight years. After that I went to Romsey and got a job in Lights Tobacconist and Confectionery which I enjoyed very well until the owner died and then, of course, I had to leave.

In the wartime, from 1942 to 1945, I worked in an aircraft factory, Vickers Armstrong, in Anglesea Road, Shirley. We made Spitfires and I did the bonding in the engines which was very interesting to do, bonding the forward bulkhead left header tank. We all looked forward to seeing it finished and going out of the hangar.

One day we were working as normal and all at once the siren went. We rushed to the shelter, and just as we got down there a terrific explosion blew up the part of the factory we had just left. We were very, very lucky not to have been killed.

After the war I went to work for Hilliers Nurseries in Jermyns Lane packing the seeds for them to take into the shop. I was there for thirteen years. After that I went to work for Mr and Mrs Attlee. He was a solicitor in Romsey and they came out to live in Braishfield at Boares Garden in The Square. I was with them eight years and then they went to Romsey to live. I didn't need to work any more because I was sixty then and I got my pension.

On the right hand side of Crook Hill as you're going out of the village there was a place where quite a few men were employed making bricks. There were a lot of wells up there and further down here in the village. When I was a schoolgirl there were wells at the door of the first cottage, Number 1, and at Number 4, where we used to draw water up in a bucket. Some people by the name of Grace who were artesian well-borers lived in Brook House and just outside in the road in the hedge Mr Grace put a tap for the people in the village to have water for all time. Everyone brought their buckets down from the top of Crook Hill and from up as far as what is now The Homestead where the Bartlams live. On Sunday mornings it was quite a meeting place for all the men to have a talk while they were getting buckets of water for their wives. Our wells were filled in when the tap was put in.

Mr Grace had a blacksmith's shop as well in those days and when I was only a young girl I used to go over and blow the bellows for him and he would give me a toffee apple for it. And when he went to town in his pony and cart I waited to open the big gate to let him go through and I got another toffee apple.

I'll tell you a joke about the Dog and Crook. In those days there were one or two lads who would play games on people. Mr and Mrs Monger were landlord and lady then, and one night when everybody was in the Dog and Crook some of the lads crawled up the back of the thatch and put a wet sack on top of the chimney and smoked everybody out. And they went and sat over on

The Dog and Crook pub in the 1930s.

the Crook Bridge then and laughed at them seeing them all come out.

Darts teams from all round come to the Dog and Crook to play in darts matches and they used to have a jolly good evening.

The Dog and Crook burned down many years ago. The fire was caused by a lady called Mrs Wilson that lived in the end house, Number 1, in those days. She was cutting her hedge with a flame-thrower, and when she got to the top of the garden she couldn't control it. It all got out of hand and went across and into a shed where Mr Monger had his car. It burnt the car out and the engine shot right up in the air and went onto the top of the thatch and burnt the pub down.

There were quite a few accidents on Crook Hill in those days because the roads weren't kept up and the hedges and trees were allowed to be overgrown. When they got to the corner they couldn't see who was coming and they just went on and they all bashed into each other. It was always happening. In those days there wasn't the Romsey Hospital. There used to be what they called a 'nursing home' at Cherville Street and they all had to go there.

There was the flower show every August in the field beside the chapel where the old peoples' bungalows are now. There were lots of tents for the exhibits, and at school we did needlework for the show and some of us got prizes and some didn't. We all went in to see who had best for the vegetables and then we would go into another tent where you could get a drink. The men would have beer and we had crisps and biscuits. The Michelmersh Silver Band would play music and we danced to it and had a very nice time.

I went to the chapel and to the Chapel Sunday School every Sunday from two-thirty to three-thirty. Around about August we had an outing which we looked forward to very, very much. We all used to love going to Swanage or Bognor and all we had to pay each was seven and sixpence. This was when I was a schoolgirl, about nine or ten, well before the war.

Gertrude Abraham in the door of her shop in the late 1930s.

Sunday School Picnic 22nd September 1923. The driver is Ernest Savage, Millie Dunford's grandfather.

The first bus we had in the village was to Romsey every Saturday and the person that arranged it was Mr Parsons who lived in Lower Street. Later we were all very excited when there was a bus started into Southampton from Kings Somborne. It was called the Empress and it used to go in every day for one and ninepence return.

There were shops in the village then. One was a very nice shop up in The Square which was run by Miss Abraham and her brother, and he used to bake all the bread and bring it down all round the village in a pony and trap. Another shop up against the school was run by Mr and Mrs Thorne where we all used to like to go and get a sherbet dab and a stick of liquorice for a ha'penny. There was also a temporary part post office in a house near the corner of Newport Lane run by Mr Dummer.

Fannie, also known as Ann or Annie, lived her whole life in Braishfield or, as she would have said, " 'Tis Brashfield!" Her wartime service brought her into contact with many young Spitfire pilots one of whom took her up for a trip across the countryside, an act which earned them both a reprimand. Her hearing was irreparably damaged as a result of a bomb blast. She cared for her parents, Joe and Lucy Holbrook, until their deaths in 1966 and 1970. She died in September 2003.

95

The Braishfield Country Fair
Roy Hughes (1922–2003)

1976–1982

Roy and Simone.

One Sunday in May 1975 when I was having my afternoon tea on the lawn John Saunders who was a friend of mine came to see me. John was born in the village; he was a general builder, very capable in everything he did and very well liked by everybody that knew him. The idea he proposed to me was that Braishfield should organise a country fair to show the old crafts being practised and ancient machinery working on one Saturday afternoon for the edification of the village and their friends. I thought it was a very good idea.

It so happened that John had recently seen Robert Corry, a farmer at Pucknall, who had indicated that he had plenty of room on about twenty-seven acres quite apart from a huge field on the other side of the road which could take five thousand cars.

We never thought we would fill this area but in fact this was just about the space we needed. So we already had the venue and a car park, a good start.

We decided to hold the fair annually on the first weekend in June for charitable purposes. The whole idea was to give a good day out for all the family and very good value for money with enough variety to suit all tastes. There would be as many things for children and wives as there were for men, as we knew perfectly well that the men would gather round the steam machines and talk about them for hours on end.

From the first day we started off with four people, John Saunders, Monty Olden, Robert Corry and myself. John would arrange for all the craft displays, which was to be a much bigger job than he thought initially. I was going to arrange local administration and the money, and Robert Corry was going to look after the site. Monty Olden, Master of the Hursley Hambledon Hunt, was going to organise the heavy horses and their transport from different areas of the country, and the horse shows in the ring. Now you don't put on a show like this without having some financial

Two 'yokels' in the stocks on the 3rd Braishfield Scouts' stand at the fair. On the left is John Tuppen, the District Scoutmaster, with Alan Beusmans, one of the leaders, on the right. Pam Saunders is walking through the ring in the middle distance.

backing. At that time the hunt, which had their headquarters in the village, was looking for some publicity because they were having trouble from people who were against hunting. They lent us six hundred pounds to get going and we paid them back at the end of the first year, giving them a pretty healthy donation in recognition of their contribution. They put on a big ring show with the hounds every year.

John was building an extension to my house at that time; we had ad hoc committee meetings almost all day long. We did nothing but talk about the fair. We soon realised that a secretary was essential and Pam Saunders, a cousin of John's, was a willing volunteer, and in the second year of the fair we asked Bob Walker, one of our shopkeepers, to act as treasurer. These six comprised the full committee. Eventually, we asked Colin and Enid Oliver to deal with publicity, and Ted and Sheila Still to make the tremendous number of signs which were going to be needed. They did a remarkable job.

Our first handbill advertised craftsmen, a cavalcade of agricultural antiquity, vintage vehicles and machinery, and a full ring programme of sporting displays and entertainments. Admission for the first year was sixty pence. We flooded most of South Hampshire with Braishfield Country Fair posters. We went round to many of the garages and big shops and some building societies to put

BRAISHFIELD COUNTRY FAIR

FOR ALL THE FAMILY

PUCKNALL FARM, BRAISHFIELD, ROMSEY, HAMPSHIRE
6th & 7th JUNE 1981
FROM 10 am DAILY
EXTENSIVE FREE PARKING — LICENSED BARS — RAC SIGNPOSTED
CONTINUOUS RING PROGRAMME — SPECTACULAR ENTERTAINMENT
COME EARLY!

exhibits of country crafts in their windows and gave free tickets to the people who worked there. Possibly the most important factor was TV and radio coverage. John Saunders went to South Western House to be interviewed for BBC South, and in 1978 we were approached by the BBC TV series 'The Getaways' who wanted to make a half hour fly-on-the-wall programme about the organization behind the fair and the two days of the fair itself.

We soon realised that what we thought was going to be quite a small affair for the village was going to turn into a very large event indeed. We were going to need help from a number of organisations for the many things we could not organise ourselves.

The Southampton Lions operated the restaurant and bar in a massive marquee which was superbly equipped and staffed and hugely popular with the thirsting masses. The beer was refrigerated, something unknown at shows such as this. The Romsey Lions manned the car park. The sight of that huge area full of vehicles was a delight for us organisers. We made large contributions to both Lions clubs in return for their assistance.

There was to be one entrance on the road by Hawkes Farm, which was in the charge of Peggy Parsons and Simone, my wife, who organised volunteers to take the money. As Braishfield is a small village with narrow lanes we realised we were going to have traffic problems and I was given immense help by Geoff Baird who at that time was a Superintendent of Police at Winchester. The police took a large part in the fair and there were always at least six policemen on site. They looked after lost children and kept an eye on the traffic problem.

Craft exhibitors were allowed to sell anything related to their particular trade or craft and a percentage of any profits that they made would be given to the fair. They were given a free sandwich lunch. At one point we had twenty-six steam tractors on show all requiring water and coal to keep them going over two days. We provided the coal, another hefty expense which we hadn't thought of when we envisaged the show. But the biggest bill every year was for tentage.

The showring itself was very large; it had to be to take twenty-six odd heavy vehicles. There were times when the smaller ring programmes seemed to be almost lost in the vast area. The ring programme, which started at ten o'clock on Saturday and Sunday, included winching and threshing displays, a German beer music band, the parade of steam, water divining, parade of vintage tractors, horse drawn vehicles, vintage cars and motor cycles, the Hursley Hambledon Hounds, a fire brigade pump display, parade of old and ancient commercial vehicles and scruff dog racing.

Now scruff dog racing was probably the funniest thing that we had ever put on because the dogs were not racing dogs at all, just ordinary pooches. They would be put into boxes, just like greyhounds, and set off running after a hare. It was really so hilarious how some of them used to stop and go back and others would start running and keep running and we would never see them again.

The Reverend Boothman was asked if he could take a short service at 2pm on Sunday before the ring show started. Everyone who was standing around the ring sang the hymns and it made a nice part of the show.

A steam-driven stationary baler at the Braishfield Country Fair. Stationary balers were made during the 1930s and used until 1950 when pick-up balers came from America. The stationary baler needed five men to work it and the straw had to be pitched six feet up into the hopper with pitchforks. A pick-up baler requires only a driver as it takes the straw direct from the swath. Here straw is being re-baled where the knots have slipped. The men look pretty fed up with the bad tying.

Rita Stitt, Lillian Martin, Joan and Bill Parsons, Girlie Old and Linda Martin by a traction engine.

The steam exhibits were organised by Derek Isaacs who at that time lived at Woodley. Rog Rogers of Yokesford Hill did a wonderful job with the stationary engines; he had eighty-nine of them, all working full blast on different sorts of jobs. Tom Andrews, who was in charge of old tractors and implements, runs a large heavy vehicle repairs business at Shootash. Motorcycles, cars and commercial vehicles were looked after by Norman Sykes of Awbridge, and the trade stalls by Malcolm Hack who lives in Lower Street.

It would take a full day to be able to see and assimilate everything of interest in the show. Among the crafts demonstrated were corn dollies, hand-fired enamels, heraldry (coat of arms and family names while you wait), ironwork (decorative ironwork by blind craftsmen) and glass blowing. We had a coppersmith, leatherworkers, a wheelwright, blacksmith, water diviner, a cooper and a rake maker. There was jigsaw making, hand spinning, machine knitting, feather craft, wood turning, glass engraving, chair caning, and sheep-shearing done by a local policeman using hand clippers. The sheep sometimes objected strongly!

There were displays of muzzle loading, archery and clay shooting, an exhibition of coins and medals, ceramic sculpture and a display of sewing machines from 1850 to 1930.

We weren't sure what to expect on the Saturday morning of the first show but very early on there was a queue of vehicles stretching from the show ground, right through the village up to Romsey Road and beyond. The weather was so warm for the first fair it was an absolute heat wave and this greatly helped its success. For the second fair the weather was terrible. I remember sitting in a caravan at ten o'clock when the show was due to open watching the rain coming down in torrents. It stayed like that all day and I was astonished to see the great British public turning up to see a country fair when it was coming down in sheets.

The mornings of the two days of the show were very busy and started about 3am for the organisers. The village hall committee provided those people who had been up all night and working with a traditional cooked breakfast, something that we all looked forward to at about nine or ten o'clock. The fair paid for this breakfast and the profit went towards building the new village hall. The village hall committee also arranged a toy balloon race and an immediate raffle for bottles of whisky with tickets at one pound each. Large sums of money were made for the village hall building fund from this novel idea.

The Boy Scouts sold the fair programmes and also operated a coconut shy which made in excess of six huundred pounds towards their funds, an amazing sum.

Braishfield is twinned with the village of Crouay in Normandy; they made several visits to sell cheese, wine and Calvados from their own tent at the fair and we all took part in games of petanque during their visit. The twinning committee took on the hard work of assembling and collating the five thousand copies of the eighty-page fair programme for which they were paid by the fair and this greatly helped their funds.

We had a hot air balloon for two years, and the first year I elected to

Alan Smith trying the stocks which were run by the 3rd Braishfield Scouts.

Margaret Stewart spinning hair from an Old English Sheepdog, 6th June 1981.

go for a trip. We landed in a tree in a small copse and the pilot managed to free the cage by using the burner. The balloon and much of the tree landed safely in a nearby field. Bob Corry had a trip the following year but his landing was not as exciting as mine.

On the Saturday evening following the first day's show we had a barbecue and barn dance which was held under cover in a huge barn close to the show ground. Tickets were two pounds each (one pound twenty-five pence for exhibitors) and it was very popular. It was organised by Bill Henderson, the publican at the Wheatsheaf Inn. He roasted a whole pig the first year and the following year we had barbecued sausages, chops and steak.

The first two shows in 1976 and 1977 each attracted in excess of seven thousand people. We thought attendance would probably stay at that level but the word got round that there was an excellent country fair to be seen in Braishfield and each year new people arrived in addition to those who came year after year. The RAC and AA arranged signposting from the other side of Winchester and from the outskirts of Southampton and the New Forest and it was almost impossible not to realise that there was something exciting happening in Braishfield. One year over twenty-five thousand people turned up. At the last show, however, there were only about fourteen thousand and it was then that we decided not to continue anymore because we were starting to make a loss. It was very nice at the end of the fair to know that everyone had enjoyed themselves but that wasn't the end of the story. We had to clear everything up, pay all the bills and already we were working on the programme for the next year's show.

I would like to thank all our wives who for many years had the country fair spilling out of their homes. They must have been fed up with it and yet they played the game and they helped us without stint. Sometimes people say, "How about organizing another country fair?" It can't be done. There are too many regulations to be met now and the fire has gone out of our bellies. More importantly, John Saunders is no longer with us. This article is a tribute to all those who took part, but in particular to John, whose idea it all was. Rest in perpetual peace, John. When we all meet again in the hereafter maybe we can do it again on a large, heavenly cloud – not forgetting the car park!

Roy, Simone and their children, Tony and Caroline, moved from London to Braishfield in 1965. Roy was an insurance consultant and Simone taught French at La Sagesse in Romsey. He was for many years Secretary of the Braishfield Village Association. As a couple they played a leading role in the twinning of Braishfield with Crouay in Normandy, a link helped by the fact that Simone was born, and has her family, in Bayeaux.

Fire at the Dog and Crook
Eric Irish

1939–2000

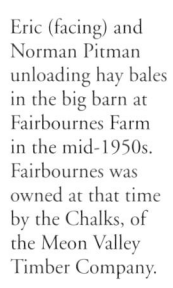

Eric (facing) and Norman Pitman unloading hay bales in the big barn at Fairbournes Farm in the mid-1950s. Fairbournes was owned at that time by the Chalks, of the Meon Valley Timber Company.

The Dog and Crook on fire, 21st April 1955. In those days if a pub failed to sell beer for more than one night it could lose its licence. The village rallied, a marquee was set up, glasses and beer borrowed from the Newport and Wheatsheaf and 'The Dog' stayed in business.

When I came to the village in October 1939 I came as a nursemaid! I was fifteen and working at Eastleigh Works driving a steam hammer in the carriage works. My father was works foreman at Farrs, the contractor, and they wanted him to go to Egypt on a job they were bidding for. I could go with them if I could hang on until the end of November, which I was keen to do. My aunt, who was living down at Fairbournes and returning to work, asked if I would look after my three year old cousin Daniel while I was waiting – so I became a nursemaid. When the job in Egypt fell through

I started working on the farm for Mr Pitts and stayed there twenty-four years. When he died in 1946 the farm was bought by Mr Cook from Wellow. He asked me to stay on and that's when I got interested in gardening because he turned the farm into a market garden. There were always plenty of staff at Fairbournes Farm, permanent as well as casual. Most of the casual workers were from the village although some used to cycle out from Romsey. And there were a few German prisoners of war.

It was while I was working for the Cooks at Fairbournes Farm that the Dog and Crook burned down. They had three boys who were very interested in gymkhana and show jumping and they had gone off for the day to a show somewhere. Norman

Eric in the milking shed at Fairbournes Farm in the days before the milking parlour. A portable machine was placed between the cows which were milked one by one.

Pitman and I had just brought the cows down Kiln Lane and into the cowshed when Norman saw a lot of black smoke down the bottom of the orchard and we thought we'd best go down and have a look. When we got there we saw the garage burning and as we went over the fence the petrol tank on the car exploded and sent flames up on top of the thatch. We went straight into the pub to see what we could do and started carrying the furniture away. We were the first two in and, by the time we had carried out the three-piece suite and several other items, a lot more men had arrived and we were able to save most of it. I remember pushing the piano out from the bar. Afterwards the furniture was stored in the shed I kept my tractor in on the farm so it could be kept under lock and key. There were several boxes of twelve bore cartridges up on the little ledge at the top of the stairs, which we just ignored without thinking of the danger, and when the fire was finally out they were still there! Mrs Monger, the landlady, was wandering around with two huge fruit bowls full of florins and half-crowns, one under each arm. She was worried to death about her money and didn't seem too bothered about the furniture. Her husband was up at Kiln Lane in the little orchard they had there feeding his pigs and chickens. Luckily enough it all happened after closing time. Pub hours in those days were from 10am to 2pm so it must have been around three o'clock in the afternoon. The flames leapt up the thatch to the top of the roof, then they were drawn down between the chimney stack and the edge of the thatch and started burning underneath, which is why the firemen had such a job to put the fire out. They had to claw a three-foot thickness of thatch off the roof and it was several days before it was entirely out. It was a great pity to see the old pub destroyed because it had so much character.

It was quite a lot of fun because we didn't realise the danger we were in at the time. I know we had several drinks afterwards! We learned later that the fire was started by Mrs Wilson in the cottage next door burning weeds off with a blow lamp beside a creosoted fence which caught fire and, as it was hot April weather in a dry spring, away it went.

A galvanised roof was put on pretty quickly and the pub opened again. When it was rebuilt they made it bigger because in the old pub you had to go down three steps to get into the cellar where all the beer was kept in barrels. During the winter Mr and Mrs Monger would serve the beer with wellingtons on as the cellar was under water.

She was a very smart old lady who had been a cook in service in her younger days. Everything had to be spotlessly clean. Every day she used to scrub the floor in the pub in the early morning before opening, then again after lunch and before opening in the evenings. It was just the bare boards, no lino or carpets, and it was all white and scrubbed. When the new pub opened up she was never happy with it. We talked her round to having darts and she was quite pleased when we won a trophy and she had her photograph taken with her darts team. She was quite a character.

The next owner of Fairbournes Farm was Mr Chalk who stayed for only three years and returned the land back to general farming. Mr Howells, who was blind, was the last farmer I worked for there before the Garretts came. I left in 1963 to work for Tom Graham looking after the pigs at

The Dog and Crook just after the war. Ted Monger's shed, where he kept his car, is in the middle of the picture.

The winning darts team in the 1960s. Left to right: Stuart Law, David Cox, Eric Irish, Sidney Sawyer, Bernard Cook. Seated: Mildred Monger with the trophies.

Velmore Farm in Chandlers Ford and later I took on the cows as well. After seven years he offered me a job at Farley Farm which he also owned, as he was going to sell Velmore, and we moved back to the village.

Years ago the main occupation in the village was farm work. All the farmers had at least three men working for them; one or two of them like Mr Owen of Elm Grove Farm had six or seven. Girlie Old was one of the workers there. It's all mechanisation now and farms can survive employing only one man.

There were three shops in the village at one time and vans came out from the International Stores and Home and Colonial. There were deliveries from the butchers and fishmongers in Romsey. Over the years the shops closed down one by one. The old post office on the corner of Newport Lane went many years ago, then the old village shop at The Square. The General Stores by the school was the last of the old shops to close and now the one in Hill View is gone. When you consider we had three shops and a post office in the village it really didn't hurt much to go shopping in those days.

But it's a hard life running a shop. My wife's father was the only Sunday newsagent in Romsey. All the outlying places had to come to him to get their Sunday papers. He used to go down to the shop at five o'clock in the morning on a Sunday, and he wouldn't get home until six or seven in the evening. On weekdays he would open at half past six to catch the workers going to Strong's Brewery who bought their cigarettes, snacks and morning paper from him.

He had one day off a week when his daughter would take over the shop.

I'm still not recognised as a villager, although we've been here sixty-two years, but my children are because they were born here.

Eric married Jean in 1949; they have three sons and two daughters. For many years he worked on the farms belonging to the Grahams, first at Chandlers Ford then at Farley. His farming career was completed with Mr Corry at Fishponds. A long standing committee member of the Braishfield Horticultural Society his expertise is in great demand at the annual flower show where he is a consistent prize-winner. Eric and Jean live and garden in the centre of the village.

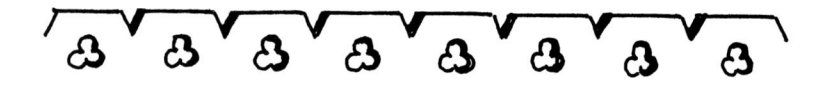

A Glimpse of the 1970s
Cherry McCall

1970–1980

When we first arrived here thirty years ago it was a common occurrence to see the Hursley Hunt riding through the village. Other occasions we much enjoyed were on Boxing Days when the late Dorothy Bacon who lived opposite had the Michelmersh Band playing carols in her garden.

The flower show, which was abandoned during the war, was restarted in 1978 by Margaret Old. We all had a very busy time making flower arrangements and cakes and sandwiches. My husband entered some vegetables and won first prize for his courgettes, his being the only entry in that class! The show was held in a large marquee at the recreation ground as the old village hall was not big enough and in the evening a barn dance took place with bales of straw provided for seating. It was great fun and a huge success.

In those days there was a reasonable bus service and we had three shops and a village policeman. There was, of course, much less traffic, perhaps a quarter of that today.

My husband, Philip, remembers that one of the more remarkable events of recent years was the discovery by Michael O'Malley of the famous Mesolithic site and house at Broomhill above Fernhill Farm. Philip went up once or twice and did some spadework. On one occasion he was given the opportunity to take out a microlith from a sieve and was told that he was the first person to handle it since it was struck about six thousand years before.

A microlith is a very small flint tool about 2 cm long used as an arrow tip or set in a grooved haft of bone or wood to act as a knife or scraper. Details of the site have been written up in the volumes of Current Archaeology Number 63 (1978) and Number 69 (1979).

Cherry and Philip McCall moved to Braishfield from Southampton in 1971 a few years before Philip retired.

Beaker from Broom Hill

An example of Bronze Age pottery found at Broom Hill. At Broom Hill there is evidence of intermittent settlement from the late Paleolithic right through to Saxon periods. The site is particularly noted for the range and quality of its Mesolithic flint tools.

Organisations

1950–1987

The opening chorus in national costumes at a Braishfield Seven concert in the early 1950s. Left to right: Back row: Janet Cottle (Scotland), Rita Stitt (Wales), Joan Parsons (Spain), Ena Glister (Holland). Front row: Mollie Russell (Norway), Shirley Cottle (United States), Girlie Old (China), Peggy Parsons (Austria).

A WI Garden Party, 'Dutch Day', at Orchard Cottage in the summer of 1954. Left to right: Standing: Mrs Eastwood, Wendy Eastwood, Jennifer Eastwood, ?, Joyce Alford, Mrs Windibank, ? hidden, Mrs Head, Barbara Bell, Elsie Cottle, Peggy Parsons, Mrs Steiner (in shadows), Miss Bacon, ?, ? hidden, Maisie Benham, Janet Cottle. Sitting: Angela Alford, Elizabeth Benham, Mary Windibank, Edna Cottle (back), Susan Benham (front), Jean Benham, Jean Head, ?, Isobel Teece.

The Braishfield Brownies in 1963, taken in the school. The white cubicle behind was the school office. There was a Brownie pack in the 1930s which was discontinued before the war. It met in the Church Room on Saturday afternoons. Founder members were Doris and Ena Dewey, Girlie Old and Mollie Russell. It was re-formed by Peggy Parsons not long before this photograph was taken. Left to right: Back row: Standing: Rosemary Fielder, Sarah Boothman, Janet Cook (Tawny Owl), ?, Jean Rolfe, Penny Thelwell, Peggy Parsons (Brown Owl), Susan Benham, Hannah Boothman, Diane Fare, Marilyn Payn, Penny Butler. Middle row: ?, Mary Turner, ? Suzanne Parsons, Pam Lawson, Mandy Woods. Front row: Doreen Fielder, Anne Byrne, Elaine Turner, Polly Darlington, ?, Denise Fry, Sally Musselwhite, Patsy Bell, Phyllis Woods. The two children in their nighties are dressed to perform the song, 'Dream-makers'.

A Braishfield Seven concert with the Folk Group around 1970. Left to right: Back row: Girlie Old, Shirley Smith, Janet Cook, Joan Parsons, Edna Cottle, Peggy Parsons, Rita Stitt. Front row: Patsy Bell, Sarah Boothman, Lucy Baker, Sally Musselwhite, Sue Benham.

111

The Mothers' Union on the Rectory lawn in the 1970s. Left to right: Back row: Vera Rampley, Mrs Elkins, Lily Proom, Irene Trueman, Joan Boadella, Doreen Veal (Preston), Mrs Nash. Middle row: Gladys Tinker, Winifred Butler, Mary Boothman, Ruth Alford, Betty Pearce. In front: Ruby Parsons.

The Braishfield Cubs in 1982/83. Known faces: Richard and Kevin Light, Christian Thomas, Robert Saunders, Christopher Hackman, Tom Quarendon, Ben Kington, Daniel Tuppen, Jim Ross.

The presentation of bibles to the Junior Church on 21st April 1985 at the Braishfield United Reformed Church with Shirley Smith (Leader) and Rev Alan Jones (Minister). Back row: Richard Light, Stuart MacMasters, Mark Anstey, David Anstey, Kevin Light.
Middle row: Victoria Snelgrove, Lee MacMaster, James Light, Adam Fildie, David Fildie, Allan Holyoake. Front row: Joanne Light, Laura Snelgrove, Emma Snelgrove.

The Choir in 1986/87. Left to right: Back row: Sarah Ransom, Elizabeth Fielder, Tim Wilson, Kate Quarendon, Ian Puffett, Daniel Richards, Rebecca Freckleton, Peter Quarendon, Lucy Freckleton, James Kington, Nick Shepherd, Sarah Boothman, Sid Scorey, Hannah Boothman, Malcolm Fiddes. Front row: Gemma Fiddes, Roanne Fiddes, Ruben Fiddes, Daniel Kington, Greg Lowe, Ben Kington, David Irish, Stuart Gurr.

The Braishfield Music and Drama Society (BMADS) rehearsal in the Church Room for 'Toad of Toad Hall' in 1986. Left to right: Alan Gurr, Tim Wilson, Peter Quarendon, Tony Lowe, Chris Balchin.

Cast photograph for the BMADS production of 'The Wizard of Oz' in 1987. Left to right: Back row: Tom Quarendon, Daniel Kington, Clare Chisholm, Victoria Balchin, Stuart Gurr, Sonia Gurr, Jody Ayres. Middle row: Roanne Fiddes, Kate Quarendon. Front row: Helen Chisholm, Gemma Fiddes, Debbie Ayres, Ewen Ross, Joanna Ross, Alexandra Balchin.

Filming 'Worzel Gummidge'
Kate Marshall

1977–1980

The popular series 'Worzel Gummidge', which starred Jon Pertwee as Worzel and Una Stubbs as Aunt Sally, was filmed around our village about twenty years ago. Pucknall Farm in Dores Lane became Scatterbrook Farm, the home of Worzel's friends Sue and John and the location of the barn where Worzel kept his exchangeable heads and cooked up many of the shenanigans that amused children on a Sunday evening. Ten-Acre Field, where Worzel scared the crows when he wasn't cavorting about with Aunt Sally, is on the right as you drive up the hill out of Braishfield towards Kings Somborne. Jon Pertwee's distinctive bright green TR7 became a familiar sight around the village and is something that I remember well.

Kate, aged ten.

I was only eight or nine years old at the time so my memories of living in

The day Worzel came to life in the field above Bailey's Down.

Alan Smith, Una Stubbs and Jon Pertwee in a moment of relaxation during filming of 'The Scarecrow Wedding' in Michelmersh Barns which were used as the location for the Crow Man's house.

a place frequently taken over by a film crew are slightly hazy, but snippets of detail emerge from the fog from watching videos of some of the episodes.

The production crew made use of a multitude of willing extras to be found around the village. In one particular episode, which centred around a country fair, I was amazed to catch a glimpse of Shirley Smith, Barbara Bell, Peggy Parsons and Roy Hughes egging on Aunt Sally, who was merrily throwing coconuts at Worzel in an attempt to knock off his head.

The village school featured in one or two episodes, and included the children who were there at the time. One story line filmed in the school involved Worzel clambering onto the school roof to look for one of his heads. The hilarious consequences caused a very young Amanda Bartlam and Christopher Richards, amongst others, to laugh raucously and get told off by a teacher who did not notice Worzel's legs dangling outside the window.

I do not recall how Mrs Shepherd, the headmistress, felt about the show-biz intrusion into the all-important business of drumming the three Rs into the sixty or so pupils who attended the school at the time – not kindly, I suspect. The accuracy and speed of mental arithmetic produced when Mrs Shepherd, adorned in one of her smocks, pointed in one's direction and boomed, "Nine times six!" was astounding. The school was renowned locally for its prowess on the netball court. Despite the terrifying exterior Mrs Shepherd had a huge

Aunt Sally shying coconuts at Worzel's head watched by Mr Peters. Known faces: Left to right: David Parsons is the bandsman (he is a member of the Michelmersh Silver Band), Jenny Lichfield, Roy Hughes, Shirley Smith, Patsy Bell.

soft spot for the children. I suspect that the angry tirades were simply caused by the fact that she cared deeply that each and every one of us should do well in the big wide world outside Braishfield School. If the school performed well at some competition or other, and at the end of every term, she would bake the most mouth-watering caramel shortcake. I have not since found any that tasted so good.

Another village location was All Saints' Church and several village members appeared in an episode called 'Choir Practice'. Worzel and his singing head had become involved in the village choir during Harvest Festival and inadvertently released several field mice which proceeded to eat the produce adorning the church. I found out from one of the real choir members who were involved in this scene that the field mice appeared to have been drugged and had to be prodded to make them move in anything like a convincing manner. Grenville

The winning netball team of 1981. Left to right: Back row: Amanda Bartlam, Lucy Freckleton, Helen Watkins, Elizabeth Harris. Front row: Wendy White, Ruth Fielder, Jackie Fowgies.

Richards remembers having to shoot the mouse scene about seventeen times before the director was happy with the result and recalls that, whilst by the end he was starting to tire of trying to look scared of lethargic field mice, Aunt Sally was professional to the end, speaking her lines as if it was the first time that day that she had to do so and producing knitting from her handbag between shots.

I appeared in part of a Christmas episode that was also filmed in the church. It consisted of school children singing a Christmas carol whilst Sue and John became involved in some escapade, no doubt the result of some high jinks caused by Worzel himself.

I was overjoyed to be released from school on three consecutive days in order to film the thirty second slot, despite the fact that we were only filmed on the third day. On the first two days we sat around in the Church Room waiting for our talents to be called upon and perfecting the carol we were required to perform. We had to wear warm winter clothes and the outsides of the church windows were decorated with fake snow. Eventually we recorded our carol and then were filmed singing whilst John and Sue enacted their scene. I remember their words to this day: Sue – "Come on!"; John – "Where to?"; Sue – "Never mind where to, just come on!"

I was paid eleven pounds eleven pence per day for my troubles and opened an Abbey National savings account with what seemed to me to be the small fortune of thirty-three

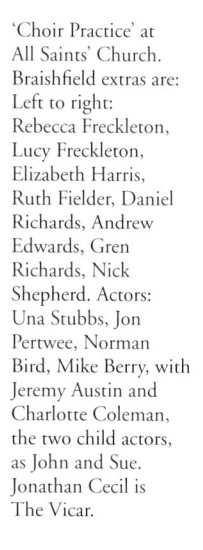

'Choir Practice' at All Saints' Church. Braishfield extras are: Left to right: Rebecca Freckleton, Lucy Freckleton, Elizabeth Harris, Ruth Fielder, Daniel Richards, Andrew Edwards, Gren Richards, Nick Shepherd. Actors: Una Stubbs, Jon Pertwee, Norman Bird, Mike Berry, with Jeremy Austin and Charlotte Coleman, the two child actors, as John and Sue. Jonathan Cecil is The Vicar.

pounds thirty-three pence. I remember I kept looking at the savings book in wonder at the amount of money I had.

Watching some of the episodes can be a disturbing experience as you sometimes find yourself launched from one end of the village to the other in a matter of seconds. For example, John and Sue frequently manage to run the two miles from Pucknall Farm to the road to Kings Somborne bewilderingly quickly and are not remotely out of breath afterwards. In one scene Worzel Gummidge and the Crow Man somehow managed to have a conversation at normal volume whilst one of them was standing in Church Lane and the other outside Pucknall Farm, nearly a mile away.

Kate Quarendon came to Braishfield in 1975 when she was four years old and lived opposite the school which she attended. She moved back to the area after university and now lives with her husband, Lucas, and son, Max, in a cottage in Newport Lane.

The War Years
Robin Merton

1939–1944

Mrs Houghton-Beckford in 1940 with her children Robin (seated centre), Adrian and Caroline.

I was eight years old when, in 1939, my family moved to Braishfield to live at the Manor. At the outbreak of the war our family was living with my maternal grandmother in Winchester. Convinced we were to be the victims of the Luftwaffe if we stayed in the city, my grandmother was prevailed upon to buy a house in the safety of the countryside. Braishfield Manor was available so willy-nilly that was where we went.

It was a wonderful place to live and a child's paradise, with extensive grounds and mysterious shrubberies in which to play. There were stables with ample room for our ponies and my mother's horse. We also had a trap pulled by a rather wilful mare called Victoria. After one or two interesting and hair-raising journeys, the last of which resulted in my mother and my brother being thrown out onto the road, this petrol saving device was abandoned and Victoria and the trap were sold to a more competent driver. The shooting-brake which replaced this team was a more reliable form of transport but just as exciting. My mother crashed it at least once.

The Vauxhall Bedford shooting brake by the front door in 1939. "My mother crashed it at least once."

The Manor was a very comfortable house and not nearly as big as it looks, but it did require a big staff to run it. After all this time I cannot remember exactly what indoor domestic staff there was, nor sadly their names. We certainly had a cook and at least one daily. Nanny, a rather vinegary spinster, held sway in the nursery, and I think there was a nursery maid as well. There was a splendid gardener called Mr Biddlecombe who lived in one of the Pitt Farm cottages. He was a tyrant and woe betide little boys who picked his tomatoes and soft fruit. Out-witting Mr Biddlecombe was a favourite activity. He kept the place in apple-pie order and we were never short of fresh vegetables and fruit. In one of the garden sheds there was a large apple loft and sand boxes for storing root vegetables for the winter. Mr Barnes, who was the general factotum and who helped in the stables, was a valued member of the household.

The house had at one time been lit by acetylene gas, which was generated in a smelly out-building on the bank behind the kitchen, but by the time we came to live there this form of lighting had been replaced by electricity. There was a state-of-the-art anthracite boiler in the cellar for hot water and the central heating. This roaring monster had an automatic stoking device, fed from a hopper and driven by an electric motor turning an

Mr Biddlecombe in the Manor gardens.

Archimedes screw. Very modern in 1939.

It was an idyllic life for us children but escape from the war was not possible. We were well aware of the air battles going on above our heads. Sometimes showers of hot spent cartridge cases and belt clips fell in the garden much to our delight but to the great alarm of the adults. I do not remember any bombs falling on Braishfield but I think that occasionally spent and unexploded anti-aircraft shells fired by the guns defending Southampton fell on the village. To the best of my knowledge no one was hurt. From the terrace in front of the house one had a perfect view of the dogfights over Southampton. One could see the barrage balloons above the docks and the shell bursts in the sky and of course the smoke and, by night, the glow of the fires on the ground. We also saw our fair share of enemy aircraft in various states of disrepair, one of which crashed just to the north of Upper Slackstead between the road and Gudge Copse. That caused great excitement.

The village smithy was a source of great wonder. There was a huge hand-operated bellows and a furnace from which the smith plucked red-hot iron to be shaped on the anvil with ringing blows from his hammer. Occasionally we were treated to the sight of a wooden wagon wheel being fitted with a new iron tyre, a task requiring two men to fit the tyre and hammer it into place amid the smell of charring wood. And then there was a hiss of steam when the tyre was quenched to make it a tight fit. Now the smith and the smithy have gone and with them a part of village life.

My father and my stepfather were both in the services and serving over-

Adrian Houghton-Beckford in 1939 mounted on his pony with George Barnes at its head. George Barnes lived in Chalk Pit Cottages.

The Home Guard in 1945 – Braishfield Platoon, 10th Battalion Hampshire Home Guard. Left to right: Back row: Pte Arthur Burdon, Pte Stuart Irish, Pte Eric Irish, Pte George Randall, Pte Geoff White, Pte Reg Randall, Pte Arthur Smith. Second row: Pte Charles Parsons, Pte Ken Chapman, Pte Arthur Rose, Pte John Mason, Pte Frank Matthews, Pte William Parsons, Pte Alfred Beeson, Pte Oswald Goulding. Third row: Pte James Fielder, Pte Frank Dunning, Pte Archie Tanswell, Pte Bert Cawte, L/Cpl W Minns, L/Cpl Guy Reg Old, Pte Stan Parsons, Pte George Fielder, Pte Bernard Cook. Front row: L/Cpl John Hoddinott, Sgt George Dummer, Sgt Tom Ross, P/Sgt Fred Chapman, 2nd Lt William Saunders, Lt Fred Gosden (MM), Cpl Ron Pitts, Cpl Fred Jordan, Cpl Fred Parsons, Cpl W Mills.

seas. The household's participation in the war effort was not great but I do remember threading endless rolls of scrim into camouflage nets laid out on the lawn. My mother drove a WVS tea wagon to various military and industrial sites in the surrounding countryside, much to the alarm and despondency of other road users. As far as I know the van survived without incident. On one occasion I went with her to an aircraft factory near Chattis Hill, just to the west of Stockbridge. The only trace of the site now is the road sign, 'Spitfire Lane', which is still there.

As I remember it the weather seems to have been much more predictable in those days. It was hot in the summer and cold and snowy in winter, but I expect I can only remember the good bits. The autumn hedges were full of blackberries and hazelnuts and the fields abounded in mushrooms and we were all dragooned into picking rosehips which were sent off to be processed in to a syrup rich in vitamin C.

Getting about was not a problem for us boys. We had our ponies and all our friends had stables so parking was not a problem. We also had our bicycles, which were a great boon, and if all else failed we went on foot. On one occasion my brother and I bicycled to Winchester via Baileys Down and Farley Mount, a round trip of some fourteen miles; and it was a very hot day.

In the early days of the war, the Local Defence Volunteers were much in evidence. One of their rallying points was at the crossroads opposite the Manor where my brother and I went to watch their activities. Later they became the Home Guard and were issued with khaki uniform and rifles, but before that they turned out in a motley collection of 'uniform'

The Hursley Hunt setting off from Braishfield Manor in 1939. The huntsman, Fred Gosden, leads off with Robin Merton as first whip.

with whatever weaponry came to hand. As D-Day approached military activity increased and many of the roadside copses contained dumps of war materiel and ammunition. By the time the invasion started my family had left Braishfield and moved to Stoney Cross in the New Forest.

I have very happy memories of our time in Braishfield. My wife and I occasionally drive through the village and then the memories come flooding back. They were happy days in difficult times.

Robin Merton lived at the Manor with his mother, Mrs Houghton-Beckford, and his younger half-brother, Adrian, and half-sister, Caroline. He spent his working life as a professional soldier in a cavalry regiment. On leaving the army as a Lieutenant Colonel he became the Regimental Secretary and Museum Curator at the Home Headquarters of the Royal Hussars in Winchester, where he and his wife now live.

The Glister Sisters
Ena Ninnim & Maggie Batchelor

1940s–1950s

Ena (left) and Maggie.

Our house was next to the Dog and Crook; a lovely little cottage, two up and two down. Ena was the first to be born there, then came Tom and Richard. Mum already had three so that was six of us children in that little house, but we managed. Father was away in the army at the time. There was no running water and we had to go across the road to a tap which was used by three other cottages. Mrs Holbrook lived in one of them and her daughter, Fannie Holbrook, still does. Then Mum and Dad were allocated one of the council houses in Common Hill Road and we moved there in 1940. We had electric light instead of the lamps we had at Crook and, although we didn't have a tap in that house either, there was a well which served four houses and a copper in the wash house at the back which had a separate bath area. All the water had to be carried in from that well. Mother stoked the copper every Saturday night. You then bailed out the water and everyone had a bath. There were outside loos, inside plumbing came after the war.

Monday was wash day. We went to school at nine o'clock in the morning, and Mother would be just getting out the galvanized baths and putting them on the kitchen table. One she washed in, the next one she rinsed in and then the last one was the blue bag one for the final rinse. The copper would be going for hot water – and the steam! – the kitchen would be full of steam. She boiled the sheets. We would come home at about four o'clock and she would be just about finished and scrubbing the kitchen floor. We all had to either stand outside or tiptoe through into the other room. And the back door step was always scrubbed on Monday, and the front one chalked white. The mangle was outside and there would often be two or three bucketfuls left to put through when we got home. We always had cold meat and mashed potatoes on Monday.

During the war there was a gun encampment up at the top of the village behind the church where Merrie Meade is, in those fields going up to Fernhill. Every time there were raids in Southampton we were absolutely deafened by the big anti-aircraft guns. They were all camouflaged and dug into big trenches so you couldn't see them. Some Americans were billeted up past Fernhill and our brothers used to go up there and come back with chocolate and all sorts of things. Ampfield Wood was full of Americans and they came down the fields to the pub. They were very friendly and always gave us children sweets. The village people were encouraged to invite them into their houses to have cups of tea and chats and there were two especial ones that came to us. One played the guitar and we sang 'The Yellow Rose of Texas' and other songs, too. They were probably not there that long, just a few weeks, but it seemed a long time to us.

Just before D-Day there were trucks parked in the village all down the lanes, wherever there were trees, and all through the woods; army lorries, big gun transports and troop carriers. Going to school we could see them, all camouflaged, waiting to

Playing on the recreation ground in the late 1940s. Left to right: Richard Glister, Dave Old, Reg Fielding, John Fielding, Ray Ward, Ron Jordan, Janet Fail, Paddy Glister, Peter Fielding, Jim Fail, Arthur White.

go to Southampton and then across to France.

Several bombs dropped in the village, probably because of the guns being there, and we all felt a bit vulnerable. Mother was on her own, Dad being in the army at the time, and when the air raid siren went we all rushed over to the next door neighbours, Mr and Mrs Dewey, taking our pillows and blankets and slept under their big kitchen table. Mother probably felt safer with the neighbours. We snuggled down under there and, when the all clear sounded, we would get up, half asleep, and go back to our own beds.

Mr Dewey, a great village character, was very prominent in our lives. He was kindest when he was a younger man but as he got older and more crippled he was a man to fear because he grumbled at you. He enjoyed having discussions and arguments and liked to sort out the politics of the village. He rode a bike and later, when he became more crippled, he had what we called a chariot which was a three-wheeled carriage he pedalled with his hands and kept his sticks in the back. He had an allotment where the allotments are still. There was a sandpit where the garage site is and he let his chickens run into it. He and his wife had six or seven children and they lived in The Gardens when the children were small. She was always busy and seemed to hang hundreds of handkerchiefs up singly on her washing line.

Most villages had a road man and the hedges and ditches were really well maintained when there was a local person to do it. Mr Gritt did it for a long time and before him Cedric Musselwhite's father. One of Mr Dewey's sons, Ray, was our last village road man. He was really good at his job and he always liked a good old natter. They would all be horrified to see the state of the hedges and ditches today.

Many children were evacuated to the village from Portsmouth during the war. Nearly every house in the village with children had an evacuee billeted with them. Even though Mum had all of us she still had to have one, a boy. Because there were more children in the village school the Womens' Institute Hall opposite April Cottage

Mr Dewey with his bicycle.

127

was used as a classroom and all the big boys went up there for their classes. The headmistress at the time was Mrs Dane and there was a male teacher who came from Portsmouth. Ena was very fond of Mrs Dunster who was the Junior teacher. Miss Euston was her headteacher and she stayed for a long time. She was there when Maggie started school and so was Miss Morrie and Mrs Saunders. Mrs Benham was the school secretary first and went on to teach. Whenever there was a vacancy she filled in; she was a lady who could turn her hand to most things.

Our school dinners were brought up in a van from Romsey and the teachers did everything. They dished the meals up and they watched in the playground, helped by the older girls. One year, in 1947, we had an awful lot of snow and because we lived so close we still had to go to school and only Miss Euston was there. The children that lived in the council houses were the only ones who could get to the school. Ena was very chuffed because she was allowed to look after the infants and she taught them for about a week. She was about twelve or thirteen.

The school was heated by old big black stoves with chimneys going up, and the coal had to be heaved in every night. Mum was the caretaker and cleaner and she went down about six o'clock in the morning to get the fires going and again late at night to stoke them up for the next day. It was hard work. Our socks were put round the guard rail to dry. It was very cosy and we could always get warm and dry. The screen that goes across to divide the big room is still there and the teacher sat in a big high desk above you.

Peggy Euston on holiday in 1941. She was headmistress of Braishfield School after Mrs Dane.

Mrs Dewey with two of her children.

Every Friday we used to catch the bus or ride our bikes into Romsey for cookery lessons at the Alma Road School. The boys went to woodwork in Romsey, too. It was a morning out.

You left Braishfield School at fourteen and went to school in Romsey. Ena went to the one behind The Plaza which we called 'The Cowsheds'. She was the first one of the family who did the extra year when they changed the school leaving age from fourteen to fifteen. From then on everybody did one final year at Romsey. Maggie started at the new school in Greatbridge Road in 1957 when the leaving age from Braishfield School was changed to twelve.

There were three shops in the village. The post office in the bungalow up on the corner of Newport Lane was run by Mrs Dummer. The telephone box was opposite like it is now and the little brick built place behind was the telephone exchange. The baker's shop plus a little grocery shop was where the Gurrs live beyond the War Memorial on the left. It was run by Mr Fred Abraham and his sister Gertie who was lovely. They baked the bread in the bakery at the back. Our sister Kath worked there on Saturdays before she left school and Ena took over from her. We used to deliver the bread in a real old Trojan van which had an old klaxon horn that went 'beep-beep', going up all round Farley. Mrs Bailey took it on in the 1950s, then it was the Quixleys, then the Masters family and then Mr Green. There was a third shop which was an off-licence as well opposite the school. It was run by the Thornes when we first knew it. They lived in Worsley Lodge where the Quarendons are. The shop was in that little bit of a passageway which connected it to

Romsey Cadets on parade on the recreation ground in 1944. Left to right: Jim Glister, Arthur Sweet, Maurice Freegard, Jeff Musselwhite, Cedric Musselwhite, Eric Freegard, Sid Mason (head just showing at rear), Fred Biddlecombe, John Webb, Horace Chant, Romsey Leader Hunter.

Red Cross group in front of the Red Cross Cadet float at the Romsey Carnival in the 1950s. Left to right: Mrs Baker, Barbara Bell, Ruby Payn, the Cadet Officer Betty Smith, the Commandant Maisie Benham and Mildred Hayward.

the house the Thornes' daughter lived in which is where the Paynes live now, so it was all linked up together. Mr Greenwood who became president of the club came to live in the big house when Mr Betteridge took the shop over. Later on the Almys ran the shop and then Mr Gadd. The last village shop in Hill View Road which closed in 2000 was built in the 1950s by Eddie Simms when he came out of the army. Maggie worked in the post office for Mr Crosland who had bought it from him.

There was a lot to do in the village when we were growing up. Ena remembers the youth club which Mrs Russell, Mollie's mum, used to run in the Church Room. We have bibles presented from some American church. The Americans tended to give us things like that when they were over here. All the local boys, including our brothers, Maurice Freegard and Arthur Sweet, were in the army cadet force which met in a hut they had built at the bottom of the Rec. The guide company which Ena belonged to met in their own hut down at Crampmoor where Woodley Village Hall is. The guides were run by Mrs Nora Loader and her sister, Mrs Doris Bunting. Mrs Bell and Mrs Fare used to pile us into their cars to take us to play tennis at Romsey tennis courts which was a really exciting thing to happen.

There were square dances at the WI Hut, especially when we had all the evacuee children in the war, and a film show every Saturday morning. Mrs Payn and Mrs Smith ran the Red Cross at the school later on which Maggie really enjoyed when she was a teenager in the late 1950s. Their

The Braishfield Congregational Chapel Sunday School in 1951/52. Left to right: Back row: Mrs Katy Old, Pam Gritt, Sylvie Chapman, Paddy Glister, Dick Glister, David Old, Reg Fielding, Jimmy Fail, John Fielding, Shirley Cottle. Middle row: Jean Head, Edna Cottle, Pete Fielding, David Head, Victor Gritt, Arthur White. Front row: Janet Fail, Margaret Gritt, Jean Fielding, Joan Fielding, Norma White, Maggie Glister.

dances at the WI Hut were the highlight of our young teenage years. There was always a gaggle of girls, and a gaggle of boys behind, when we came home in the dark. Everyone had to fundraise to pay for our badges and suchlike.

The chapel and the church had very good Sunday Schools on Sunday afternoons which all the children went to and Dad used to take us for a walk afterwards, up the road and down Kiln Lane. We had a Sunday School outing every year. Most times we went to Swanage but we went to Hayling Island quite a bit, and Weymouth. The chapel and church went together for a few years. The Sunday Schools were very big because families were much larger then and most children went from the age of five or six until they left school. Maggie went to the youth club on Friday nights in the church hall for ten to sixteen year olds. Mr Boothman was in charge and somehow managed over twenty children. He had beetle drives and whist drives and we played snakes and ladders and ludo. Beetle drives were the highlight because

The Congregational Church (now the United Reformed Church) Sunday School outing to Sandbanks in 1969. Shirley Smith (left) has her son, Alan, on her left with Deborah Gardiner on her right, and Anthony Gardiner in front of her. Maggie Batchelor (right) is holding her son, Malcolm.

The Braishfield Seven Group including 'the backstage boys' in January 1964 on the stage of the WI Hall. Left to right: Back row: Joan Parsons, Rita Stitt, Edna Cottle, Peggy Parsons, Janet Cook. Middle row: Ena Ninnim, Mollie Russell, Margaret Old, Shirley Smith. Front row: Bill Parsons, Rusty Smith, Charlie Dewey, Elsie Cottle, Stan Parsons, Bernard Cook, Ray Weedon.

it got very noisy. The Reverend Boothman always played and never cheated which was something we watched to make sure he got it right. We never went anywhere else, to be honest, and it was so exciting to go up there with a group of youngsters and there was this one poor man coping with us all. He did admirably and somehow we were always going home laughing. The boys used to get up to all sorts of mischief but he was back there again the next week.

The Braishfield Seven concerts started just after the war. The original seven were Janet and Shirley Cottle, Mollie Russell, Girlie Old, Peggy Parsons, Heather Foxcroft, and Ena. Rita Stitt joined soon afterwards and later on Joan Parsons, Pam Gritt and Peggy Vear, because in some years we had more than seven. Maggie came into it for two or three years with Edna Cottle and Jean Benham. It was originally put on for one year as an entertainment to raise money for the Sunshine Home for Blind Babies but once started it continued right up to the 1970s. The backstage boys were Stan Parsons on painting and electrical work, because he was an electrician by trade, Charlie Dewey as prompter, and Bill Parsons on rope pulling for the curtains. Rusty Smith helped backstage later on. Mrs Cottle played the piano for us because most of the time we rehearsed in the front room of the Newport. We did every one of the concerts in the old WI Hall. Mrs Russell's son, Archie Tanswell, taped them for us on his tape machine with the big round spools and got music for us if we wanted different tunes. There were various drummers, the main ones being Graham Doe and Ray Weedon.

The Coronation Day Parade on 2nd June 1953 passing the school. "Ena was a horse and had to push Shirley Cottle in a pram."

A highlight of our year was potato picking in the fields which belonged to Mr Owen at Elm Grove Farm because we had a week, or sometimes two, off from school. Girlie worked for him and Henry and George Randall, and Bill Randall's dad, Reg. We went up there on our bikes and got paid sixpence a day which was a lot of money then. We had to work hard, picking them up in a bucket and putting them into sacks. Everybody had an allotment and you ate what you grew in those days. They took up the whole of that field right down to the telephone box. The school had one next door to our Dad's, all marked up into eight patches, and the boys used to go out and work on it which was good for them.

Mr and Mrs Harold Randall who lived along Common Hill had pigs up at the top of their garden. Most people kept pigs. Mum had one during the war and so did Dad. There was always bowling for the pig at the village fete, and you actually got a pig. Our Dick got it two years running. The pigsties were at the top of our garden and we had chickens as well which was a good way of having meat and eggs during the war.

In Coronation year, 1953, we had a really big event in June. There was a carnival with floats and we all dressed up in costumes. Ena was a

The Future Braishfield Seven float in the Coronation Day parade. Left to right: Elizabeth Stitt, Edna Cottle, Maggie Glister

133

'The Crazy Gang' with their band. "There were so many on floats there was no one to watch!"

horse and had to push Shirley Cottle in a pram. The Braishfield Seven had a float for their young friends and relatives and Maggie was a fairy on it. There was an open double-decker bus with people up on the top level with the band. All the children were given a New Testament. We still have ours together with the Coronation mug presented to us by Lady Bacon.

The parade went down past Elm Grove Farm towards Pucknall and all round the block ending up at the recreation ground. Boxer Old was there with his old trombone, Mr Fielding had a side drum and Mr Gritt had the big bass drum. These three people were all that were left of the old village band which Mr Scorey used to talk about going back before the First World War. On Boxing Day and on fete days they marched through the village, and they played at the flower show when it was held in the field opposite the Wheatsheaf. There was a flower show up at Farley, too. We entered and had to name the flowers. Dad bought Maggie a doll made by Mrs Rampley which she's still got.

An old lady, Mrs Toulmin Smith, bought the house next to the shop in Common Hill. She was a real lady and Dad used to do the garden for her on Saturday mornings. She played the piano and when we went into her kitchen she always said, "Would you like a drink and a biscuit?" The kitchen was ever so small and there was a bath in there with a lid on it which she used for putting things on, except when she had a bath. We loved going with Dad because to have a sweet biscuit or a chocolate biscuit was really a treat. Dad used

The Braishfield School netball team of 1948. Left to right: Back row: Shirley Cottle, Ann Goulding, Elsie Holey. Middle row: Heather Webb, Rosemary Love, Ella Sweet. Front row: Ena Glister, June Biddlecombe.

to do two or three ladies' gardens. Maggie delivered a paper every day to Mr and Mrs Dummer who lived in a bungalow along Common Hill. They had topiary birds cut out of bushes in their garden which are still there now. She went every day and got sixpence a week for delivering their Echo.

There were whist drives in the Social Club run by Mrs Bob Old who lived in Common Hill and Ena went with Mother. All the older generation went like Mr Dewey, Mrs Boxer Old, Mr and Mrs Dummer, Mrs Williams and Mr and Mrs Bob Old. You were afraid of making a mistake because someone always told you off if you put the wrong card down. Once when Ena hadn't been playing very long she was drawn against Mr Dewey who was always very strict on what you did. She was a bit perturbed when she picked up her cards because she and her partner had the whole thirteen tricks! He was absolutely horrified to think that awful scrap of a girl had them all, but it made the highlight of the evening. Going to the whist drive was really something.

Ena and Maggie Glister were born in Braishfield, two of the eight children of Annie Kathleen and Walter Glister.

Ena is married to Les Ninnim who has an engineering business in Michelmersh. They have three children, Keith, Ruth and Sarah.

Maggie still lives at the family home in Common Hill with her husband, Jack, who is steward of the Social Club. Their two sons, Mark and Malcolm, live locally. Until 2002 Maggie was the cook at Braishfield School.

Guns and Wheels
Malcolm Norman

1959–1962

I moved to Braishfield in 1959 from southwest Scotland with my father, sister and brother. We lived initially at Fernhill Farm then after about six months we moved to Crook Hill when my father bought Craig Fad Farm which had belonged to the Ellcocks who had formerly been bakers in Romsey. My father farmed pigs there.

Peter Baker, who was about the same age as me, lived opposite, and Nigel Gould, another friend who was a little bit older, also lived at Crook Hill Farm. He later became well known as our local postman.

Peter Baker and I used to go shooting together and we had the rough shooting on Crook Hill Farm and also at Fairbourne Farm which belonged to Mr Howells. I particularly remember one evening when Peter and I were shooting on Fairbourne Farm and Mr and Mrs Howells were out shooting as well. Mr Howells was totally blind. A pigeon flew overhead and Mrs Howells told Mr Howells where to point the gun and when to pull the trigger and the pigeon fell out of the sky. I was very impressed and wouldn't have believed it had I not seen it myself.

A shooting party in the woods.

I went into the services when I was fifteen years old. A year later when I was sixteen I was home on leave for a time and built a go-kart. We used to run this go-kart up and down Crook Hill which you probably wouldn't get away with in this day and age.

One of my fondest memories was of Ted Knowles who lived up a way beyond what was the post office in Hill View. Ted owned several Scott motorcycles which had a two-stroke motor with a very distinctive sound. I can particularly remember that if Ted got one of his Scotts out of the garage and started it up I could tell it was a Scott. I used to look forward to Ted coming down through the village and over Crook Hill bridge and winding the throttle wide open to go up Crook Hill. Believe me there is nothing that sounds quite like a Scott when it's on full chat, as we would call it.

Ted Knowles in 1985. He rode motorbikes all his life right up to his death in 1994.

Malcolm Norman came to Braishfield with his family when he was thirteen years old. After his service career he lived in Scotland eventually moving back to Braishfield to run his transport business from the village. He and his wife, Angela, now live in Whiteparish.

The Football Club
Dave Old

1907–1992

The Football Club in 1961. Left to right: Back Row: Peter Fielding, Bill Byrne (chairman), Ray Watkinson, Dave Parker, Brian Parsons, Jim Fail, Arthur Sweet (secretary), John Fielding. Middle row: Melvyn Parker, Len Gritt, Brian Wood, Arthur White, Dave Old. Front row: Peter Gritt, Ray Miller (captain), Reg Fielding. All are Braishfield men except for Ray Watkinson (Romsey) and Ray Miller (Ampfield).

Braishfield Football Club was formed in 1907 and is one of the oldest clubs in the county. No matches were played during the two world wars and the club as it exists today was re-formed after the war in 1945 playing friendly matches for several seasons until entering the Eastleigh League, and then on to the Southampton League. Jeff White was a prolific goal scorer and in the 1950 season netted fifty-seven goals. The Braishfield players then were Charlie Moody, Sonner Old, Frank Dunning, Cyril Dunford, Norman Fielder, Charlie Dewey, Bill Byrne, George Beloch, Les Gwilt, Bert Proom, Bob Russell, Jeff White and Arthur Holmes.

Their most successful season was in 1960–61 when Braishfield fielded a fine side with Len Gritt netting forty-seven goals and Dave Old scoring ninety-six. This was a club record for the number of goals scored by one player in a season and still stands forty years later. Braishfield only just lost the league title on goal average to a strong Shirley Warren team. That season the Braishfield players

138

The Braishfield Football Club at the Dell in 1992 at the final of the Southampton Senior Cup. Left to right: Back row: Steve Webb (manager), Darren Challis, Nigel Noyce, Cain Sedgwick, Barry Hunt, Mark Barrett (captain), Wayne Windebank, Neville Porter, Dave Old (chairman). Front row: Bill Reid (secretary), Duncan Anderson, Graham Collins, Mark Stuckey, Mark Page, Richard Weeks, Wayne Jacobs.

were Arthur White, John Fielding, Ray Miller, Brian Parsons, Peter Gritt, Dave Parker, Melvyn Parker, Reg Fielding, Brian Wood, Jimmy Fail, Dave Old, Len Gritt, Jake Cox, Peter Fielding and Ray Watkinson. Veteran winger Reg Fielding's career started in the late 1950s and he still carried on playing into the early 1980s.

Braishfield then began to climb the ladder threading their way through the Junior League and then on into senior football and in the 1986–87 season were rewarded

Braishfield Football Club in action against Aerostructures in the final of the Southampton Senior Cup in which they were defeated 2-0.

139

The Football Team soon after the war, when the lads were all back home. Left to right: Back row: Ted Fail (linesman), Cyril Dunford, Frank Dunning, Norman Fielder, Charlie Moody (goalkeeper), Bob Russell, Gordon Old, Bill Gritt (trainer). Front row: Les Gwilt, Bill Byrne, Jeff White, Arthur Holmes, Bert Proom.

with Hampshire League status. In 1992 they reached the final of the Southampton Senior Cup but were defeated by 2-0 by Aerostructures at the Dell. Braishfield sides at present play in Hampshire League Division 2, and Southampton Senior Division 2, and the club also still runs an over-forties veterans' side for friendly matches. On the last Sunday in July each year they run a six-a-side football tournament when sixteen local villages all compete.

To show that some things don't change much in the letters column of the Advertiser a lively correspondence is reproduced here following what appears to have been an ill-tempered match during their first season in 1907.

From *The Romsey Advertiser* 15th November 1907

The Braishfield Football Club opened their season with a match against Ampfield in the field of Mr Sargent, kindly lent for the occasion. The play was of an even description, although at times rough. Half time saw 2 goals each, and the match ended in a draw of 4 goals each. Archer for Braishfield played well. As time goes on this newly formed club should give a good account of itself.

From *The Romsey Advertiser* 29th November 1907

Braishfield entertained Awbridge on Saturday in a friendly, the visitors arriving with only 10 men. At half time the homesters led by three goals to nil, and eventually, after some even and rough play, Braishfield ran out winners by 6-1. It would be better, writes my correspondent, if players, when engaged in a friendly game, would keep their tempers under control.

From *The Romsey Advertiser* Letters to the Editor 6th December 1907

Dear Sir
Will you kindly allow me through your valuable paper to say a few words re Awbridge v Braishfield team. In the first place let me say that we were supposed to have played Braishfield, not Braishfield and Ampfield, or rather pick of Hampshire. Secondly we did not arrive with ten men, only eight, playing nine till half-time (picking up one on the ground) and one more arriving after half-time. Thirdly, players losing their tempers (I suppose your correspondent refers to the Awbridge team).

I think it is time that the Braishfield Football Club induced better and more efficient men to referee their games, or am I thinking it will be a case of other teams losing their tempers. What the Braishfield team asked for they most assuredly got; for instance, they appealed for a free kick for a foul; the game was stopped for a minute or so; the referee did not know what to give, as he said he did not see a foul, but on Braishfield making vigorous claims for a free kick he (I should say) very unwisely gave a free kick, without even consulting the linesman at all. I think it would be better for Braishfield, and I am sure it would be for visiting teams, if they got a better official to referee their matches, so as players could keep their temper a bit more.

H J Pragnell, Capt Awbridge Albion FC, Awbridge, Romsey Nov 29th 1907

From *The Romsey Advertiser* Letters to the Editor 13th December 1907

Awbridge v Braishfield
Dear Sir
Will you kindly allow me through the medium of your paper, on behalf of the Braishfield Football Club, to just say a word or two re the letter in your last week's issue referring to the match played at Braishfield. In the first place the match was not reported by any member of the Club but by the correspondent in the village. With regard to the team being Braishfield, Ampfield and the pick of Hampshire, in our team nine of the men were members of the Club living in the village, and the two players from Ampfield were got at the last minute. Was not this the best thing to do rather than follow the example of Awbridge in the past and scratch matches. Those who are interested in village football know how difficult it is to be certain of a team one Saturday after another. It is quite correct that Awbridge arrived (half an hour late) with only eight men, picking up another player on the ground before starting, and another from Wellow arriving some time before half-time, and as to losing tempers the correspond-

The Football Club of the 1908-09 season taken outside the village school. The players and officials are: Back row: C Croucher, W Abraham (goal), F Webb. Middle row: M Sargeant, F Gee, W Thorpe, A Bundy and W Hooper. Front row: Fred Fielder (honorary secretary and Norman Fielder's father), F Gould, G Dummer (captain), Henry Travis (Alma Fail's father), H Marchment.

ent did not refer to Awbridge more than Braishfield, but it seems that the cap fitted. Our referee who was appointed for the match failed us at the last moment, but any referee is liable to make a mistake, and one free kick was not much to complain of, and, again, Awbridge brought no linesman to consult. It is well perhaps, for Awbridge they arrived late, only allowing half an hour to be played each way, or else they may have got from the newly formed Club a worse defeat than they received. We trust that when we visit Awbridge we shall have a good referee, and a good Awbridge team and we will do our best to give them a good game with Braishfield men.
Yours truly

F W Fielder, Secretary to Braishfield Football Club, Braishfield, December 11, 1907

From *The Romsey Advertiser* Letters to the Editor 20th December 1907

Braishfield v Awbridge

Dear Sir
Will you allow me space in your valuable paper for a word or two in reply to my Braishfield friend's letter of December 13 appearing in the Advertiser. Without making unnecessary excuses for our team's inability to win, I think given an efficient referee we should not have been beaten by more than two goals, even with nine men. I quite agree with the Secretary of Braishfield F C in getting a team to play if possible, and not scratching as other teams do. No one dislikes scratching matches more that I do, but I can say that when Awbridge

have scratched it is when they could not possibly get a team. Again the appointed referee failed them at the last moment. From what I heard after the match they could not get a referee even from Romsey to come up for them. Also making mistakes; we all know it is impossible to referee without making mistakes. As I said before what they asked for they certainly got, fair or foul means. It was not one free kick or one mistake we complained of, it was many. I can assure Braishfield that when we come there to play again we will bring a team of Awbridge players and, providing a capable referee is appointed, hope to have a ding-dong game, as I hope we shall when they come to Awbridge. In passing I notice Braishfield correspondent writes the language was simply disgusting well, I must admit this to a certain extent, providing some of the Braishfield team are included, but was he on the field or not. I don't think he was; if he was he might have come to the conclusion that there was disgusting language used on both sides, and very little football shown by either team. In the interest of the winter pass time I hope that the correspondence between Braishfield and us will not make us bad friends, and may Braishfield go ahead and win matches galore is the wish of Awbridge Football Club and members.
I beg to be, yours obediently

H J Pragnell, Captain, Awbridge Albion FC, Awbridge, December 13 1907

Dave Old was born in the village, the son of Gordon (Sonner) Old, and attended Braishfield School. After a period living in Woodley he returned to the village where he lives with his wife, Pat. Dave is president of the Braishfield Football Club, as well as holder of the club record for being the most prolific goal scorer in a season (ninety-six in the 1960–61 season). In October 2002 a surprise party and presentation was given in recognition of his fifty years service to the club.

Teams

1900–1990

The Braishfield Cricket Club before the First World War. There has been a cricket club associated with the village for well over a hundred years. Their first permanent ground was on a piece of land known as The Common, which was adjacent to the present recreation ground, where they played until the early 1930s when they moved across to the recreation ground which proved an excellent field. When they started up again after the Second World War they played once more on The Common, Mr John Hoddinott of Elm Grove having given permission, where they continued to play until the club's dissolution in 1967. The pavilion, which stood approximately where the children's play area is on the recreation ground, was in use from before the First World War until it was destroyed by fire in 1939 or 1940. The team played friendly matches on Sundays and occasionally Saturdays and took part in knock-out cup competitions. Village teams travelled to away matches by horse and cart, the only way of getting there in those early days. Here members of a victorious side are pictured on a wagon decked out for a parade through the village to display their trophy. Known faces: Back row: Charlie Grace, Cyril Grace. Front row: Douglas Hurst, Henry Doel. Driving: Bill Waters, the carter at Abbotswood Farm.

The Cricket Team in 1955. Left to right: Back row: Bert Windebank, Johnny Golding, William Hayward, Rusty Smith, Jim Jones, Alfie Knight, Ray Dewey. Front row: Charlie Smith (Rusty's brother), Ron Windebank (Bert's son), Norman Fielder, Gordon 'Sonner' Old. Their home ground, The Common, was renowned for its picturesque setting. The club began to struggle through lack of support in the mid-1960s and was eventually wound up in 1967. Village cricket was resumed in 1981 with the formation of the Newport (Tap Room) Cricket Club.

The Cricket Team in 1990. Left to right: Back row: John Massey, Paul Fowgies, Eric Philpott, Mike Allen, Geoff Bartlett, Ray Massey, Carl Evans, Mike Ransom, Tony Mawson, Dave Vine. Front row: Ewen Ross, Andy Hollett, Ian Ross, David Moseley, Steve White, Sam Massey, Mike Samways, Steve Patterson, Kevin White. The Newport (Tap Room) Cricket Club came into being when an American, Steve Shaw (known as 'The Yank'), who drank at the Newport Inn, wanted to play the game. Carl 'Bross' Evans arranged a one-off match with his New Forest pub team, The Cuckoo Cricket Club. The Newport team won and the present side was born in 1981. In 1986 Michael Hoddinott generously offered the use of a field for a permanent ground just a few hundred metres from The Common. Their pavilion is an animal shelter acquired from a local farmer.

The Newport Inn Darts Team in the public bar at the Newport Inn in the 1960s. Left to right: Back row: Gary Windebank, Alec Cottle, Rusty Smith, Johnny Coyle (captain), Johnny Wickham, Bert Windebank, Bernard Cook. Front row: Trevor Taylor, Frank Marshallsay.

Note: Memories and photographs of the football team can be found on pages 138–143.

The Landgirl
Joan Parsons

1942–1944

Joan Parsons in her uniform in 1943.

It was in August 1942 that I volunteered to join the Womens' Land Army to do, above all things, dairy farming. Goodness knows why I chose this as I was born in London and had never been anywhere near a farm or any farm animals in my life. However, in the following November I was notified to report to a farmer at Botley, but here fate had other ideas, because about three days before I was due to leave, I was informed that the vacancy at Botley had fallen through and I was to report instead to a Mr Thomas Parsons at Sharpes Farm, Braishfield.

On the freezing cold morning of November 23rd, and never having been away from home before, I said goodbye to my very tearful mother on Waterloo Station and headed for this unknown place called Braishfield. I eventually arrived at Romsey Station several hours late, the trains being delayed due to an air raid on Southampton the previous night. Mr Parsons was waiting at Romsey Station and I was taken to Malthouse where I was to be billeted, and it was here that several of the many shocks I was to receive during the coming days commenced. The first of these was discovering that the house where I was to stay did not have electricity – only oil lamps and candles. Shock number two was that there was no bathroom and the loo was down the garden! Shock number three was being told that milking started just before *6am*. I had never been up at that hour to go to work before.

However at 6am, on my first day in the land army, I crawled across the road in pitch darkness to where this unknown job of milking cows took place. I opened a wooden door and,

The cowpen at Malthouse Farm.

by the light of hurricane lanterns, was confronted by the sight of the rear ends of a long line of cows all munching away at their breakfast. Just as I stepped inside the cowshed a mouse ran across my feet – I was very nearly on the first train back to London. My three companions were Fred Parsons (Millie Dunford's father), Charley Parsons (Gordon Parsons' father) and Mr Dick White. It fell to Fred Parsons to teach me the various jobs I was expected to carry out: keeping the boiler going for hot water to sterilise all the milking equipment after milking twice a day and cleaning out the cow shed after the morning milking. Fred told me that for about a week I could watch him and Mr White do the actual milking – for which I was truly thankful. When that week was up Fred said he would pick a nice *quiet cow* for me to learn on. Her name was Cherry. I was duly presented with my milking stool, bucket and a few instructions. It was with fear and trepidation I approached Cherry, sat down as far away as I could possibly get, and very gingerly attempted to get some milk out of her. Cherry had other ideas and every now and then turned her head and looked at me mournfully as much as to say, "What the heck do you think you're doing?" and emitted a very bored "moo". After what seemed an eternity there was not so much as a teaspoonful of milk in my bucket. However Fred came to my rescue and to my amazement within a few minutes had a bucketful of milk. After a short time however I got the hang of this milking business and Cherry and I became firm friends.

It was a few months later, when I was beginning to feel like an old cowhand, that one morning a young man came to join our little team in the cowshed. His name was Bill Parsons (son of George Parsons). It is

149

no wonder if ever I am asked where I met my husband I get a very funny look when I reply, "Sitting underneath a cow".

It was December 1943 when Bill was called up to join the armed forces and, at the beginning of 1944, Tom Parsons decided to retire from farming.

The 25th March 1944 was a very sad day for me when all the cows were sold by auction and I watched them going off to new homes. I had to leave Braishfield. However I did not move very far away, just over to the dairy on Mr Pratt's farm at Michelmersh where I remained for a short time.

Meanwhile Bill had ended up being despatched to India and finally to Burma, whilst I eventually found myself on a market garden in Surrey. So instead of huddling up to a nice warm cow on a winter morning I was in the middle of a wind swept field cutting frozen cabbages to send to the London market!

Joan Pepperdine married Bill Parsons in 1949. After a few years in London they returned to the village, living at the bungalow built by Bill's father, George. She was for many years a secretary at Jermyns House working for both Sir Harold Hillier and Roy Lancaster. Joan is one of the three surviving members of the Braishfield Seven. Bill was a churchwarden at All Saints' for over twenty-five years, equalling his father's record of service. Bill died in 1994 and Joan continues to be actively involved in village life.

Sharpes Farm before the war. Reg Rogers, who lodged there at that time, is standing in the lane.

Two Village Shops
Wendy Quarendon

1975–1998

The shop used to be a part of our house, joined by a narrow corridor. When the house on the other side, Roxana, was built in about 1918 the new owners took the shop over and the doorway was bricked up. In turn, when we bought the shop after it closed, all we had to do was to un-brick the opening.

The Village Stores in Common Hill Road when it was for sale in 1987.

The shop opposite the school
When we moved into the village in 1975, to Worsley Lodge in Common Hill, the shop next door to us was a thriving business. Maureen Fielding who worked there spent most of Friday mornings packing up orders into cardboard boxes for delivery by Mr Gadd.

Our house was built as two cottages and the gardens extended to the Wheatsheaf. In 1916 the cottages were combined. While digging the foundations for our garage we found a lot of tin advertisements – for Colman's mustard, Colman's Blue and paraffin, obviously just buried in

The Thornes' shop in Common Hill Road in the mid-1920s soon after it had been built. David Marsh Thorne was a butcher in Southampton who retired in 1918 and bought The Shanty, the house onto which the shop was built in 1924.

Number 2 The Terrace, Newport Lane, in the 1980s.

the garden to get rid of them. In the past we have found lots of old bottles, too, just chucked in the hedge.

2 Newport Lane

Our daughter, Kate Marshall, and her husband Lucas bought 2 Newport Lane when they married and found that it, too, had been a shop. The little window in the front was a post box opening, and we found a blue tin sign saying 'You may telephone from here'. The door from the sitting room has two round holes in it at eye level where the people used to look through from the back room to check if there was anyone in the shop.

Wendy and Peter Quarendon came to Braishfield with their children, Kate and Tom, in 1975 when Peter resumed his research at IBM. Involved in all aspects of village life, they have recently embraced the challenge of Elm Grove Farm.

The Hunt
Sally Rawson-Smith

1951–1978

The Boxing Day Meet rides out in 1950 or 1951 from the Dog and Crook led by Commander Bill North, secretary of the Hursley Hunt. His daughter, Susie, aged about eleven, is riding beside him, her pony on a leading rein.

One of my first village memories is of the Hursley Hunt Boxing Day meet at the then thatched Dog and Crook, probably about 1951. I was riding a small pony. Captain Faber from Ampfield House was Master.

In 1957 I kept my own horse at the kennels and helped whip-in for one season when Hugh Craig Harvey from Lainston House was the amateur huntsman. Hugh later married Jean Wilson who lived at Braishfield House with her parents, George and Barbara Wilson. I lived in a hunt cottage now known as Whites Cottage. The kennel huntsman, Owen Basford, lived next door in Cromwells and the whipper-in lived in the bungalow now called Hunters Lodge. After a day's hunting, if as usual we had hacked to the meet, the huntsman would 'blow' for home while in the village to let them know at the kennels that the hounds were coming. Rita Stitt and Girlie Old were generally there to give a friendly wave.

Before John and I were married, we used to walk out with the hounds every Sunday afternoon along the

153

Hounds passing Braishfield House in 1971. Alf Dyer, mounted, is speaking to Gary Windebank. Sally Rawson-Smith is in the gateway and Dennis Topp is walking by.

MJ Rawson-Smith, Sarah Parish and Stan Reed, the kennel huntsman, walking out with the hounds along Dummers Lane towards Elm Grove.

road to Elm Grove. For many years the hounds would be exercised through the village by successive huntsmen. After John and I were married and had moved to Churcher's Barn, Owen Basford would blow his horn to wake us up when he passed by on early morning hound exercise – now the traffic would make this far too hazardous. On a moonlit night we would hear the hounds singing in their runs at the kennels. It was a sad day when the hunt amalgamated with the Hambledon Hunt and the hounds moved to their kennels at Droxford.

Albert Cobbold was the local farrier and village blacksmith. He shod the hunt horses, of course, and Mrs King's hackneys at Braishfield Manor. Mr Cobbold had a fund of stories about the village – I wish I could remember some.

After Mrs King, Neville Dent trained racehorses from the lovely little thatched yard at the Manor. He used to hack the horses to Farley Down to give them hill work. After Neville Dent, Sir Hugo Seabright had the yard.

Neville Dent's foundation mare, Rocky Road, had a filly called Farley Mount. She bred several useful event horses. One of them is my advanced

Neville Dent on Rocky Road in the 1950s.

was immediately to the right of its stable yard (now known as Colsons Barn) and almost hard on Church Lane. There was a small D-shaped garden on the other side of the lane in front of the house. The Cottage was later demolished and the site filled to form the garden for the house built much further back by my parents, Douglas and Mary Lowman. For many years the hand bier was kept handy to the church in my parents' barn.

Sally comes from a local family. Her parents retired to Braishfield and she and her husband, John, have lived here since their marriage in 1958. Sally competed in show jumping and later went on to breed horses one of which, Trust in Me, was third in the Olympic Three-day-event Trials in 1988. Sally was joint master of the Hursley Hunt in 1964 and secretary to the Hursley-Hambledon. She and John were joint presidents of the Romsey Show in 2002.

eventer, Trust in Me, who is now twenty-three years old and whom I still ride through the village.

I also remember General Ransome who lived at The Close. He had a magnificent collection of Chalk Blue butterflies of which he was very proud. In those days The Cottage

The Cottage in Church Lane.

The hunt met at all three pubs.

Top: The Hursley Hunt meeting at the Dog and Crook in the early 1940s. Known faces: Fred Gosden (huntsman), Jack Bailey (whip), George Musselwhite, Eileen Wells, Alan Jago, Madge Old.

Middle: A Hursley Hunt Meet outside the Wheatsheaf in the late 1940s. Left to right: Jane Chrystal is on the grey, the huntsman Jack Bailey, the landlord Dick Walker with his wife and son, Richard, Ted Fail (in the cap) and Gordon 'Sonner' Old.

Bottom: The Hursley Hunt at the Newport Inn in the 1970s. Known faces: Rita Stitt, Alan Smith, Elsie Cottle, Sir John Alleyne mounted on his black horse, Bally.

The Fernhill Roman Bath-House Dig
Jane Rogers

1974–1977

The completed excavation at the Roman bathhouse site before it was filled in.

In the centre of a field just south of Farley Lane and north of Fernhill copse on the brow of a hill lie the foundations of a very substantial building in brick and flint dating from Romano-British times (the third and fourth centuries AD). This building was first detected from crop marks clearly seen in an aerial photograph which was taken during a hot summer in the mid-1960s. The field was planted with a crop of wheat when it was photographed and the very distinct pale crop-marks showed a substantial rectangular building only very shallowly covered with soil. The main axis of this building was lying north to south, and it had two semi-circular bays extending eastward, and also a smaller square 'stoke-room' on its south side. The whole was clearly a substantial and significant structure. However, not until after harvest in 1974 was a beginning made upon the main work to investigate the nature, dating and purpose of the building by an excavation.

A formal scientific dig of the site was undertaken under the auspices of the Test Valley Archaeology Committee (TVAC) because the remaining walls of the building were so near to the soil surface that the building was being further damaged every time that the field was ploughed.

It was in danger of disappearing completely without its nature and function ever being known. So the dig was begun and was continued, during the summer months only, until 1977.

Because I was at that time the only member of the TVAC committee living nearby I first became involved merely as a convenient caretaker of all the spades, trowels, buckets and brushes of the excavators. At first I was an unskilled general assistant to the more experienced amateurs and to the one professional archaeologist. I would wheel barrow-loads of topsoil from the dig to the spoil-heap whenever the weather was good enough for the diggers to make progress, or else I would wash pieces of pottery and other finds in my own kitchen sink at home when the weather was bad.

Gradually I took a more active part in the excavation, undertaking substantial stages of the excavation myself, with the more professional people involved only visiting from time to time to advise and record significant features by their scientific drawings and photographs.

As the team working on the project was reduced in number, on many days I would be alone at the dig, or only accompanied by one or both of my children. For them the spoil-tip of chalk served as the equivalent of a large sand-pit. I remember most particularly the day of the FA Cup Final in May 1976 when my eight year old daughter, Zoe, and I spent that lovely afternoon on the site, with our transistor radio tuned to hear the commentary on the match at which her father and brother were spectators – and of course we both cheered heartily when the Saints scored, even though there was no one within earshot to hear us.

That was only one of many happy sunny afternoons of those summers when, more usually, the only sounds apart from the scraping of our trowels were the singing of larks and crickets as we carefully cleaned the surfaces of walls of flint or Roman brick, retrieved pieces of painted wall plaster

Left: Three intent workers: Jane with her children, Zoe and Alex, in 1976.

Right: The lily-shaped bathing pool.

from the channels of the under-floor heating system of the 'turkish' baths or even, and most excitingly, gradually unearthed the complete, plaster-lined, lily-shaped bathing pool in what was probably the least heated of all the rooms.

At one side of the 'bath suite' there was a cobbled courtyard but there was no sign of any dwelling house in the vicinity. This may have been because the house had been constructed chiefly of timber and it had never had any substantial footings like those of the bath-house, or perhaps it was at a higher point in the field which had already suffered even more damage from ploughing, so that no remains of it could now be detected even by sophisticated scientific methods.

All my memories of the dig are happy ones although common sense tells me many days must have been dull or cold or completely fruitless. I do remember that the real labour involved was such that I often returned home really tired and with aching back and knees. But it was an exciting time which satisfied all my instincts for exploration and discovery, for during every archaeological dig you have constant hopes of a really exciting find. It is just as if you were prospecting for gold, as to do it at all you must have a constant optimism that the very next spadeful of earth may be the one through which you will make a really exciting discovery.

We never did find any such notable discovery – no gold or silver hoard nor even any major find of pottery or metal – but we did satisfy our original wish to discover what this building had been for, and when it had been built and occupied.

Jane and her family came to the village in 1968 and she left exactly thirty years later. Always a worshipper at All Saints' Church she trained as a Reader, qualifying in 1997. She has led services in all the churches in the benefice. Jane now lives in Romsey and works with the chaplains at Southampton General Hospital.

The Builder
John Saunders (1939–1994)

1940s–1970s

My earliest memory is of my grandfather's enormous pig. Her name was Betsy and she was so large the doorway to her sty had to be enlarged to allow her to enter. Betsy would frighten the daylights out of me at feeding time when she would stand on her hind legs and put her front feet on the palisade around her sty. As the food got nearer she would squeal louder and get more excited and jump up and down to the point where I was convinced she would actually leap out of the sty and consume anything, possibly even me, a small boy of three years old.

John Saunders in 1984.

Almost everyone in the village kept some sort of livestock ranging from chickens, geese, ducks, pigs and goats to rabbits. They consumed all the leftovers from the house and garden and provided a much-needed source of eggs, meat or milk to supplement the rations of wartime Britain. Most of the animals required for meat, such as the chickens and rabbits, were slaughtered by the householders themselves but the pigs were usually attended to by the Vane brothers from Timsbury who would cycle along to the house and dispatch and dismember the hapless animal.

My most vivid memory of the war concerns the searchlight based at Casbrook Common. There were several of these searchlights positioned around the area. They were mounted on trailers so they could be moved around to create the illusion there were more of them than there actually were. They could fool the German bombers into believing they were surrounding a large town, possibly Southampton, when in fact they were in open country. At the end of the war we held victory celebrations in the recreation ground with fireworks and the letters VE and VJ some three or four feet high were constructed in

Left: Ducks in the yard at Fairbournes.

Right: Maurice (left) and Eric Freegard at the pig sties at the back of their house in The Square.

wire, straw and sacking, then soaked in paraffin and ignited.

Many American troops were stationed in the area at this time and all the waste food from the army camps was placed in large tubs and delivered to pig keepers by two very large, coloured GIs in an equally large and impressive American truck. These tubs of pig swill were known for some reason as 'Wembley Puddings' although I never discovered why.

With things getting back to normal I can remember the village fete held at Merrie Meade, then the home of Mr and Mrs Dunning who kept several hives of bees at the bottom of the garden. I don't think I had ever seen a beehive before so I was fascinated to see the bees buzzing in and out of the hive. The tops of the hives were propped open so I decided to have a look inside and, to get a better view, I stood on the tray and lifted the lid. For some unknown reason the bees took exception to this and came swarming out. I ran but the bees followed and I was stung everywhere, and I mean everywhere! Mrs Dunning took me into a room with a large scrubbed table where I was stripped and anointed with a 'blue bag' to the extent where I must have resembled an Ancient Briton covered in woad. Needless to say I had a fear of bees which persisted until I was in my twenties.

I remember starting school at Braishfield where the infant teacher was a Miss Penfold who could bring tears to your eyes with the edge of a ruler. There was, of course, the annual 'nit' inspection and various welfare hand-outs such as powdered milk and drinking chocolate which was, I believe, a gift from the American or Canadian government. We were all told to take a large jar to school into which was dispensed a measured amount to take home. Most of it was consumed on the way home by continually dunking a moistened finger into the contents. Free school milk was distributed each morning in third-pint bottles sealed with a cardboard cap into which you inserted your index finger. We were each issued with a straw which we would place in the bottle and then blow

The Newport Inn tug-of-war team in 1949 outside the pub. Left to right: Back row: Alec Cottle (landlord), Charlie Parsons (Gordon's father), Mike Marsh. Front row: Harry Rose, Percy Tinker of Chalk Pit Cottage (Braishfield hairdresser), Sonner Old (Rita's brother, David's father). In the background: Fred Fielder (Bill's father).

down to create a mass of bubbles. In summer the milk was frequently sour and in winter it was so cold you could hardly drink it.

Our milk at home was delivered daily and ladled out from a churn into jugs, bowls and other receptacles. This dairy operated from Awbridge and a few years later Mr Arthur Watts of Crookhill Farm started daily deliveries with a most unusual three-wheeled vehicle which could be seen each day 'put-putting' its way through the village. Mr Watts still lives at Crookhill and the dairy business was later sold to an ex German POW, a Mr Laessing of Abbotswood Farm.

My memories just after the war concern the many characters in the village, some of whom are still with us today. There were quite a few tradesmen such as Henry Travis who was the local carpenter, wheelwright and undertaker. He had a workshop in Newport Lane. George Parsons was a carpenter and builder, and the Topp brothers from Timsbury built many houses in Braishfield and surrounding villages. Dennis Harrington lived in Newport Lane and possessed an immaculate Ariel Red Hunter motorcycle and in his spare time repaired bicycles, etc.

The Newport Inn was kept by Alec and Elsie Cottle who also possessed one of the few telephones in the village. The Wheatsheaf Inn was kept by Jack Bailey, and the Dog and Crook was kept by Ted and Mildred Monger who were my grandparents. This was the centre for much of the 'black market' trade that existed towards the end of the war. It was also the venue for the Boxing Day Hunt which assembled there every year because in those days the Hursley Hunt Kennels were at Dores Lane under the supervision of Mr Gosden.

Next door to the Dog and Crook lived 'Knocker' Pottle who did the odd bit of chimney sweeping together with gents' haircutting. As boys we were fascinated by the fact that Knocker had two thumbs on his right hand. I have since discovered that this genetic deformity goes back to the sixteenth or seventeenth century when a Spanish ship, which came from an area in Spain where two thumbs on one hand was fairly common, was shipwrecked off the Cornish coast. The Spanish seamen

The Wheatsheaf in the 1950s. The photograph dates from the time Ted Bailey was the landlord. The barns at the junction belonged to the Wheatsheaf and stood where the car park is now. The oak tree, school and headteacher's house can be seen beyond.

were absorbed into the local community and thus the defect was spread.

Haircutting was also carried out by Hedley Webb who lived at The Terrace in Newport Lane. A haircut there was very much a social occasion which was followed by cups of tea or cocoa around a blazing fire to the accompaniment of George Formby records played on a vintage gramophone whilst Hedley puffed on his pipe which was lit by one of the brightly coloured spills taken from a jar in the hearth.

One of the characters who did much to keep the village tidy in my childhood was Bill Gritt. Bill was employed by Hampshire County Council as a lengthman and he was responsible for the maintenance of a set length of roadside verges. His length encompassed the village and he kept it all neat and tidy without any mechanical assistance. All his tools were loaded onto a hand cart which he would push along each day to his place of work and when he had been right round the village he would start all over again, which was rather like painting the Forth Bridge. We didn't have complaints about brambles overhanging the footpath and nettles waist high along the verges. He did a far better job than the current arrangement where a mechanical device comes about once a year and chews everything to a pulp and spreads it all over the road.

The Village Stores, opposite the school, was kept by Frank Betteridge and as youngsters we were frequent visitors to purchase batteries and bulbs for our cycle lights. Frank had a little ritual for testing each battery or bulb before sale and as the test lamp lit up Frank would always recite, "Lighten our darkness we beseech thee, O Lord", and then hand over the item. Many items were delivered to

The village shop opposite the school in the mid-1920s which was run by David Marsh Thorne, a retired butcher from Southampton. He bought the house on the left, called The Shanty, in 1918 and built on the shop in 1924. The older person standing in the doorway is Mr Thorne's son, Denzil, who used to deliver bread and groceries round the village and outlying areas as far as Slackstead, Hall Farm and Farley in a cart drawn by a horse called Peggy. Eventually they changed to a van. The signs on the fence read 'BP Motor Spirit' and 'Remember the good tea Brooke Bond'.

the shop in bulk and weighed up into one pound bags. Sugar was always sold in stiff blue bags, so was dried fruit and rice.

Most of us bought our first packet of cigarettes from the Stores which would then be shared out and smoked furtively in some secret place. I remember my first taste of the 'fragrant weed' which was in the school lunch break. Each lunchtime we would go from the school playground through the wicket gate into the recreation ground to play football or cricket, depending on the season. It was late October and at the top end of the recreation ground was the village bonfire which was nearly ready for 5th November, and this looked an ideal cover for a 'smoke'. Unfortunately we were observed and hauled before the headmistress. On the way home that afternoon my younger sister announced with great pride that she had a letter from the headmistress to my mother, to be delivered personally. I tried to bribe her to let me have it but a two shilling piece was obviously not enough.

As soon as we reached home my sister went straight indoors and I decided now was a good time to build up some credit, so I set about chopping some firewood in the hope of receiving a lighter sentence. Within a few minutes my mother called from

PT on the recreation ground in 1939. The lime trees are saplings and only the houses on the north side of Hill View have been built.

the back door. My heart sank, there was no way out, but I had chopped quite a lot of wood. "Yes Mum," I replied, whereupon she waved the letter aloft. "Is this true?" she asked. I nodded, to which she replied, "Fancy being so stupid as to get caught. Be more careful next time!" She then disappeared indoors and the subject was never mentioned again. I took this to be like a reprieve or Queen's pardon.

As young boys we did some pretty gruesome things in the school lunch-break, such as putting some carbide into a Tizer bottle into which someone added some water (produced by natural means). The bottle was shaken vigorously and then thrown some distance. Within a minute or so it exploded, but as far as I know no one was ever hurt!

I suppose the masterpiece was performed by some of the older boys who, after studying the layout of the toilet block, decided that, whilst the girls' and boys' toilets were separated by a brick wall above seat level, they were interconnected below. A long pole was liberated from the headmistress's garden to which was attached a large bunch of fresh stinging nettles. When it was calculated that the girls were all comfortably seated the pole was passed down through the last seat hole in the boys' toilet and then turned horizontally and passed along the tunnel along the row of girls' toilet seats which, you will remember, were all occupied. The screams had to be heard to be believed and although I was not involved in this episode I well remember the canings that followed.

Of course, whenever the school governors visited the school we were like little angels. As the governor entered the classroom he or she was introduced and then said, "Good morning children". The headmistress gave a nod and, as one, the whole class stood and chirped loudly, "Good morning Mrs Ashton" or "Good morning Mr Owen" depending on who was visiting.

Mrs Ashton lived at the Manor and rode a bicycle with a dress guard made from pieces of thin cord attached to the rear mudguard. She was a very smart woman who invariably wore grey clothes. William Owen, known to everyone as 'Billy' although I think this was mostly behind his back, was a large man with white hair who lived at Elm Grove Farm.

The headmistress's garden in 1933.

Billy was very tolerant of small boys who would spend most of the summer holidays following behind the binder in pursuit of rabbits. As the machine circulated round and round the field the area of uncut corn became ever smaller and the rabbits seeking cover, kept moving inwards. So, of course, did the army of small boys with large sticks who were waiting for the poor creatures to run so that we could give chase and hopefully bludgeon the unfortunate animals to death. On a good day it was possible to go home with several rabbits, unless you were on one particular farmer's land where we were ordered to put all the dead rabbits on a farm cart and at the end of the day each boy received just one rabbit. The remainder were loaded into the back of the farmer's car and sold to a butcher in Romsey. I don't think we went there again.

In the winter there was less to do so our time was divided between our catapults at the rooks in the chalk pit near the church and riding our bicycles on the village pond when it froze over. I think the worst damage from this was a couple of bent bikes and a wet leg! As we grew older we became aware that fireworks were great fun and could be lit and placed on the unsuspecting victim's window sill or doorstep. We developed a technique for lengthening the fuse to give five minutes longer to enable us to be well away from the scene of the crime before the explosion.

Sunday mornings I attended church to sing in the choir along with several other lads. The men's section consisted of Sid Scorey, who had a very loud tenor voice, Fred Abraham, who had a rich bass voice, and George Parsons and Albert Cobbold, who came somewhere in between. Fred Abraham was, for many years, the village baker with a bakery and shop at the top end of the village. I remember he drove an old Trojan diesel van which, being a two-stroke, made a strange 'put-put' sound as it toured the village.

Albert Cobbold will be remembered by many as the village blacksmith and farrier. Albert was born in Suffolk, came to the village as a young man and spent the rest of his life here. I remember just before Albert retired he was asked to trim the feet of a donkey in Romsey. They were in a dreadful state, all turned up at the front like Turkish football boots. The discomfort no doubt contributed to the donkey's dislike of being handled. Albert instructed the owner to tie the animal's head and right hindleg securely to the fence, then to lift the left hindleg whilst Albert advanced with his trimming knife. The 'moke' was having none of this so he wrenched his foot from the owner's grasp and kicked out, planting his hoof squarely in the owner's face, breaking his nose. The owner staggered around the yard holding a hand to his bleeding nose muttering, "Oh my God!" Albert surveyed the scene for a few seconds and then said, "Well that'll teach you to keep your b...... head up next time, nipper!"

Another village character was Harry Burnett who lived in Brook House opposite the Dog and Crook.

John taking part in a scene from the pageant to mark the centenary of All Saints' Church in 1955. It was held in the gardens of The Close, the original vicarage, the home at that time of General and Mrs Algernon Ransome.
Left to right: Back row: Pam Elkins, ?, John Saunders, ?.
Front row: ?, Angela Alford, ?.

167

John's grandparents' pub, the Dog and Crook, in the early 1950s. June Thomson and her then husband, David Andrews, are standing by the door.

Harry was sort of semi-retired but made a few bob from his large garden. His speciality was cabbage plants which were sold in bundles of fifty. When he'd had a few pints Harry would usually start singing, his favorite song being 'The Little Red Caboose Behind The Train'. This was rendered on several occasions at the village fete when Harry grabbed the microphone and then started to tell some rather saucy jokes. Harry could be seen on most days working in his garden wearing khaki breeks with brown leather boots and gaiters, a collarless striped shirt and, on his head, a white handkerchief knotted at each corner.

Over the years Harry and my grandfather had several arguments but they still had a mutual respect for each other and my last memory of Harry was on the day of my grandfather's funeral. Harry was standing by the roadside clad in his usual attire and as the hearse passed by he raised a grubby hand to his head to remove the handkerchief and then wiped away the tears that were trickling down his face.

My grandfather, Ted Monger, was also a bit of a lad in his day and came originally from Andover. He worked as a stud groom walking stallions from village to village. Then he worked for Bertram Mills Circus looking after horses and later served in the First World War driving a team of horses pulling gun carriages. He later worked at the Manor where he met my grandmother who was a widow from the 1914 flu epidemic. They later married and took over the Dog and Crook. On one occasion one of the customers was particularly offensive so Grandfather took him by the scruff of the neck and the seat of his pants and hurled him into the 'Crook' stream. The man complained to the police and the following day a constable arrived and told Grandfather, "You cannot take the law into your own hands," to which he replied, "If you call me what he called me I'll throw you in!" The old boy taught me quite a lot, such as how to handle a shotgun and how to kill a rabbit quickly and then to paunch and skin it.

One Sunday morning I was invited to go on a ferreting expedition at the unearthly hour of 7am. Grandfather arrived with a large canvas bag containing ferret, nets and wooden pegs, so we set off. When we arrived at the rabbit warren Grandfather took out the net and pegs from the bag and placed the nets over the rabbit holes and pegged them down. He then went round the other side and placed the ferret in a hole. My instructions were to keep out of sight but if the ferret came out I was to grab him around the neck with finger and thumb as I'd been told. Sure enough the ferret came out, so I called to Grandfather. "Grab him before he goes back", he yelled. So I advanced on the ferret. The next thing I knew the ferret had bitten my finger so I let out a cry of anguish. "Not like that," he yelled, "Pick him up from behind." I said, "Well, you never told me that," to which he replied, "Ah! But you'll remember now, won't you?" And I did.

I remember well the late Mr and Mrs George Alford who lived at the Lodge, near the Manor. Although not natives of Braishfield they were very much local characters. Mrs Alford always seemed a very motherly figure

Fairbournes Farm in the early 1950s. The Cook boys played cricket on the lawn on Sunday evenings.

and when as youngsters we went carol singing we always called at the Lodge where Mrs Alford would invite us all in to her kitchen. The good lady was usually in her apron and working, almost up to the armpits in mince pies and other Christmas fare. We were always invited to sample the mince pies which I remember were among the best ever.

Although not in the village, we were always intrigued by the POW camp, now the site of the Ganger/Woodley estate. I believe the inmates were mostly Italian and toward the end of the war, and just after, they would gather at the fence selling hand made items to passers-by. Rope soled slippers with woven raffia uppers were one speciality and various novelty toys. After the war part of the camp was used to house various displaced persons, or DPs as they were known locally. These unfortunate people were refugees from Eastern Europe, many of whom were employed in agriculture in the village, mostly on tasks such as hoeing at Fairbourne Farm which produced a lot of vegetables and was owned at that time by Mr Felix Cook.

Mr and Mrs Cook had three sons who were into show jumping and I would go to the farm with my grandfather who would prepare the horses for the gymkhana. My job was to crank the handle of the clipping machine whilst Grandfather would clip around the ponies' feet, etc. The final touch was to plait the mane and tie it all down neatly with black thread, then some boot black around the hooves and they were ready. Felix Cook had the most terrible fear of snakes, even the humble grass snake. I remember one day we were out in the field harvesting potatoes when someone shouted "Snake!" and before you could hardly blink Felix was up on top of the cab of the lorry. The poor snake was killed and later taken to the farmyard where the Cook's eldest son, Gordon, and myself decided a post mortem was in order. It was discovered that the snake's last meal was a frog so Gordon took the grizzly evidence to show his father who was just about to start the afternoon milking. Felix fled in terror and was so ill he had to go to bed for the rest of the day, leaving Gordon and I to help finish the milking!

As we reached our teens we were all enthralled by the exploits of the late Bert Cawte because, like all boys, we were fascinated by motorcycles. Bert was always a bit of a daredevil who we believed could go faster than just about anyone we knew, in fact it was said that he only had two throttle positions fast and even faster! On a still night you could hear Bert's Triumph Twin coming up the Braishfield Road sounding like the winner of the TT.

One fateful night, however, Bert was coming towards Braishfield

Boxer Old and Derek Isaacs with Boxer's traction engine and threshing machine in the early 1970s. The 1910 Wallis and Stevens seven-horsepower traction engine was called 'Boxer's Beauty'.

when a car came out of Sandy Lane at the crossroads causing serious injury to Bert and his pillion passenger, proving that the crossroads is not a new problem. Bert recovered to a degree but sadly he lost his sparkle and then we grew older and got motorcycles of our own. We too used the Braishfield straight as a racetrack where we watched the speedo for the needle to reach the magic one hundred.

Braishfield has had its fair share of characters over the years and I suppose the most well known was the late Reg 'Boxer' Old. Boxer always retained a sort of boyish sense of fun right to the end of his life and he'll always be remembered for his many exploits. Legend has it that in his youth he built an aeroplane which was constructed from odd pieces of wood and tarpaulin and powered by an old motorcycle engine. I gather the trials were going quite well and they were starting to get 'lift off' when the landowner whose field they were using for test flights came along and put a stop to further development fearing a fatal accident. According to my father, he and Boxer were involved in the village Gunpowder Plot. I'm not too sure of the details but it seems the end result was an explosion and fire at the village sandpit.

Boxer and his father spent many years touring local farms with a traction engine and threshing machine and, of course, as youngsters the arrival of this equipment drew us like a magnet. All the equipment was hitched together when it travelled along the road. At the front was the traction engine which provided the motive power. Hitched to this was the threshing machine, then the bailer, followed

The ratcatcher in the 1940s displaying his catch.

by the elevator, and lastly Boxer's car. The threshing was carried out during the winter from ricks which had been constructed at harvest time. These ricks were usually full of vermin so a fence of wire netting was placed around the whole operation. When the rats and mice emerged they soon fell prey to a couple of eager Jack Russells, who would quite happily dart in and out between the machinery killing anything that moved. Boxer spent much of his life in agricultural contracting on whatever machinery was to be found. He was just a natural born engineer.

My first memory of Boxer goes back to when I was six or seven years old. It was at the village fete on the

Threshing straw for thatching near Woolley Green farmstead in 1990. Wilf Fry from Kings Somborne, who worked with Boxer, was the 'brains' behind the outfit. He has worked on threshing machines in the Braishfield area all his life. The machinery has been modernised as much as possible so that the outfit can be worked with just three people from the rick. Years ago a team of ten was needed.

Boxer Old and his traction engine, Beauty. The photograph dates from the mid-1970s as the wheels have rubber caps made from old tractor tyres flattened out and stuck on to the existing metal ones. This made for a more comfortable ride in Boxer's later years.

recreation ground. Boxer had made a working model of a traction engine which was always on display and surrounded by a crowd of boys between the ages of six and sixty! Boxer later went on to make a small tractor and a mechanical hedge cutter, in fact I think there were few things he could not make or mend if he really put his mind to it.

As the years passed the trusty traction engine was pensioned off and replaced by a large International Tractor and as time changed Boxer owned one of the first combine harvesters in the area. In later years Boxer could not resist the fascination of steam so he acquired 'Boxer's Beauty' and together they were a popular duo at steam rallies throughout the south. Whilst going to one such rally Boxer was interviewed by a local radio reporter who taped the interview from the footplate. The interviewer asked, "What is it you find so fascinating about steam engines?" Back came the reply in a rich Hampshire accent, "Well. See, steam engines is a bit like women, once you starts muckin' about with 'em, you can't leave 'em alone."

Upon Boxer's passing we took him to his resting place on a cart behind Boxer's Beauty. I think Boxer would have appreciated that. The sadness of the occasion was perhaps tempered by the beautiful array of floral tributes that surrounded the coffin in the afternoon sunlight. As the procession neared the church Beauty let off a haunting whistle which brought tears to our eyes.

I later remarked to Norman Goodland that Braishfield had lost all its 'characters'. He replied, "When yer old enough ta think loike that, yer probably one of 'em yerself." Perhaps he's right?

First published in the Braishfield Village News in five installments between December 1988 and August 1989.

John Saunders was born and lived all his life in Braishfield. A builder and handyman, he must have, in his time, worked in almost every house in the village. His legacy was considerable. The Braishfield Village News was his brainchild as was the Braishfield Country Fair, the first of its kind in the country. John also suggested the building of a new village hall and found the land on which the hall now stands. He died in 1994 leaving his widow, Freda, son, Robert and daughter, Jill.

The Saunders Family in 1892 outside Butcher's Farm which was near the village pond.

Buildings

1500–1855

Broom Hill Cottage in Lower Street is a sixteenth century timber frame, thatched cottage with painted wattle and daub and brick in-fill.

All Saints' Church at the turn of the twentieth century. The church, designed in the gothic manner by William Butterfield, was consecrated in March 1855. The clock tower was added in 1902 to celebrate the coronation of King Edward VII.

Elm Grove from the garden in 1905.

The Shanty in 1923 when it was owned by David Marsh Thorne, a retired butcher from Southampton. He built a shop onto the house in 1924 which continued to trade until 1988. In the late 1920s the house called Roxana was added on the other side of the shop. On the bench are his wife, Rose, and their daughter Beatrice. Their sons, Denzil and Norman, are by the door. The Shanty was renamed Worsley Lodge in the 1930s.

Orchard Cottage, a brick and thatch cottage, in 1933 with Bert and Peggy Cawte by the front door. The eyebrow windows under the thatch are a local characteristic.

The front elevation of Fairbournes Farm in the early 1950s. It is one of the oldest farms in the village.

Far Left:
The Congregational Church communion table in the 1930s decorated for harvest and lit by oil lamps. It is now the home of the United Reformed Church which was formed when the Congregational Union of England and Wales amalgamated with the Presbyterian Church of England in 1972.

Left:
Joyce Old (Alford), Millie Parsons (Dunford), and Bill Parsons in school uniform in 1934 at Fairbourne Place, their grandparents' home. Fairbourne Place has many typical local architectural features. The slate roof is shallow pitched, the ground floor window has a segmental arch above, the first floor window directly under the eaves is a Hampshire casement window which has no vertical bar, the timber framed porch has a gable over-hang.

3 The Terrace in Newport Lane in the 1980s, one of a row of cottages built at the beginning of the nineteenth century. Pam Shepherd (born Gritt) with her two children, Monica and Robin, is in the front garden.

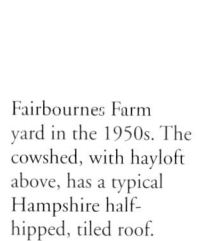

Fairbournes Farm yard in the 1950s. The cowshed, with hayloft above, has a typical Hampshire half-hipped, tiled roof.

Hall Place, formerly Hall Farm, in 1964 after extensive renovation by the new owners, Robin and Philippa Sheppard. The core of the existing building dates from the sixteenth century. This was the site of a major fourteenth century medieval manor and remains of a thirteenth century chapel were found in the garden in 1974.

The Verger
Sidney Scorey (1892–1989)

1890s–1980s

Early Years
We all looked forward to the festive season with its holiday from school, and to the village Christmas tree and tea party, and also the prize giving for regular attendance at both church and chapel. They were very happy occasions. There were several groups of lads going round the village singing carols, a custom which in later years on that scale was forbidden. Myself and my brother with two more lads made a group and we had some very enjoyable evenings. At the end of our tours we met to share out and mostly it came to a very fair amount each. The village band went around playing carols, various marches and dances. My father was a member and later I became one too.

Christmas was a time for family gatherings. The turkey was on very few tables as part of the Christmas fare. Geese were popular owing, no doubt, that they cost less to rear and fatten as they could be turned out on stubbles after harvest to look after themselves. A fair number of cottagers kept a few poultry, and the odd cockerel or two would be fattened for the Christmas dinner. In some families beef was the choice.

Sid Scorey, the verger at All Saints' for over fifty years, with processional cross outside the church in the late 1980s.

Our family consisted of Mother and Father, myself, two younger brothers and my sister. Our Christmas dinner was roast beef, gravy, potatoes, home grown vegetables, followed by Christmas pudding – good plain and wholesome food. Tea followed: bread and butter, jelly and currant cake. In many Braishfield homes of that day there were large families and wages on the farm were low. How they fared I can hardly think. My father was a hoopmaker so our standard of living, for those days, was fairly good and for several years we killed a pig for home use which gave us a supply of good home cured bacon. Our neighbours at that time were an elderly couple, Mr and Mrs John Travis. She was a dear old lady

The Wheatsheaf and Braishfield Road in the snow in the 1920s. The oak trees on the left hand side of the road are gone now. It used to be a landmark and a place for people to meet "by the oaks".

and for several years she came along on Boxing Day morning with a large mince pie for us. It was the usual custom at Christmas to hang up our stockings and we received a small present of maybe gloves, mittens or socks (something warm for winter) and perhaps an orange or a small packet of sweets, and everyone in their own way helped to make it an enjoyable time.

Almost the only form of lighting was candles to go to bed and a paraffin lamp for living room use. Heating was chiefly by logs and coal, usually more logs than coal. Cooking was done in an oven heated with similar fuel. Bath-time in winter was taken in a zinc bath by the fire and then to bed. The road, being of rough material and worn in by traffic, our boots had to be of strong material with nails in the soles, and the girls' shoes had protectors in their soles. Clothing was a contrast with today: it was waistcoats instead of pullovers. No school meals: children living at a distance brought their own and had a long and wet journey to and from school in the winter days. It meant walking, as cycles were fewer then than they are today, but we all seemed happy.

In the longer days came the Sunday School treat, which was held in a field near the chapel, with tea, games, races and a cricket match led by the vicar, Reverend Porter, who was a good player himself and played regularly for our village team. In later years, when Mr and Mrs Pepper came to Jermyns House, the Sunday School treat was held there, and later still we took our annual day at the seaside.

In the early days of my school life the headmaster was Mr Benwell, followed by Mr and Mrs Clark. They were in turn succeeded by Mr and Mrs C H Carpenter who remained for some years after I had left school. The post office was situated just on the top of the hill known then as Scorey's Hill. From what I have been told, a Stephen Scorey came from Michelmersh about 1855. As well as running the post office he was appointed parish clerk of the newly built Braishfield Church. After his decease his wife carried on for a while. In those days there were three bakers in the village – William Fielder, Frank Fielder and Caleb Abraham, who also ran the village shop. Well-boring and sinking found employment for some, a prosperous business being carried on for a number of years by Mr James Grace and his sons near the Dog and Crook. Small farmer and coal merchant was George Saunders who lived near where the War Memorial now stands. John Travis, his son and grandson, were carpenters and joiners and the village undertaker. Brickmaking and burning were carried on for a number of years at Crookhill, a man named Pritchard being in charge. There were two local carriers to Romsey – Frank Fielder and Mrs Dummer. By the pond was an old thatched cottage occupied by a family named Pottle. Their son, who was a cripple, went

George Saunders' cart at the corner of Braishfield Road and Dummers Road a few years before the War Memorial was built on the site. The board on the cart reads, 'George Saunders Coal Merchant Hire Carrier Braishfield'. George Fielder is the boy standing in the middle on the cart.

181

The local landscape in the early 1900s as Sid would have known it. Many more people were employed on the land. In this view of Paynes Hay Farm, Len Gritt's grandfather, James Rogers, is in the foreground. The elm trees on the horizon, once a common sight, have now entirely disappeared.

on Saturdays to Winchester with a horse and van, taking various produce and people.

Quite a number of villagers kept a pig and fattened it for home consumption, as we did. The pig killing was an annual event and there were two men in the village who would kill and cut them up – George Saunders and Henry Fielder. Their charge was one shilling and sixpence. After salting we took the long sides of bacon to Caleb Abraham for drying, unless a form of pickling was desired. Lovely bacon it was too.

My Working Life
I left Braishfield School at the age of thirteen years. In March 1905, leaving on Friday, I commenced work the following Monday for Mrs Bently George at Chirk Lodge near Romsey. My duties were to clean boots and shoes and knives; assist in the garden; also to do a small butter round in Romsey twice a week. My wages were five shillings a week and a tea daily. For a while I walked the three miles but later got a cycle which was a great help. I stayed there just over two and a half years and then, following financial difficulties which meant the cutting down on staff, I was dismissed. They offered me employment in the garden and looking after a horse at a farm they had taken for their son but it was only temporary. That meant my going on the farm and I did not like that class of work. I stayed on for a while, until one day I was in

a big field by myself, weeding corn and whistling as I worked, when the farmer came along to me and said, "You are not doing enough work. You can't work and whistle too." I told my father that I was not happy. He asked if I would like to go with him hoopmaking and I said I would. He told the farmer who said he would not let me go. My father replied, "I shall be here to see he does leave. Any nonsense from you will be met."

My first hoopmaking began near Michelmersh Church in 1908. It was by going to work with my father that I became involved in church work as in 1906 he had been offered the position of parish clerk. After my apprentice days were over I mixed hoopmaking with other work such as gardening and, when extra help was required, hoeing, haymaking and harvest, always returning to hoopmaking, that being my regular occupation. Parnholt was a wood of about seven hundred acres which I knew from my schooldays. It was given up to the growth of timber and underwood – hazel, ash, birch and willow. There was the annual sale of underwood and annual fall of timber. An acreage of underwood would be cut once in seven or eight years. In the timber line quite a number of oaks were felled in early May and the bark on them would be stripped. Our name for it was 'rhining'. The trunk was stripped and all branches of any

Felling giant trees by hand. Harald Neville is on the left and Gordon 'Sonner' Old of Braishfield is on the right.

size. The bark was tied in bundles and conveyed to a tan yard in Middlebridge Street, Romsey, to be soaked and used in connection with the treatment of leather. Charcoal was also burnt, and a fair amount of oak posts for fencing and rails were prepared. Some timber went to Travis & Arnold, Eastleigh.

After the purchase of the underwood in late September or early October wood-cutters would start to sort out and prepare it into what it was suited for, and the poles for our hoopmaking were laid in heaps. For a long time, hoops were sent away in straight bundles to be steamed by hot water and bent to shape. My great grandfather, on coming to Braishfield from Durley, found a way of bending by hand. My grandfather, my father and his brothers, save the youngest, were hoopmakers. I was the last. I enjoyed the work. It was fairly hard and most times it meant long walks but I was very fond of the woods. My last hoops were made near my home, where Boares Garden is today.

This work was not only carried out in Parnholt Wood but in many places throughout the area: hoopmaking chiefly, but also hurdle making for sheep cages for feeding hay to the sheep in the fields. Hurdles have now changed to a larger form and are used as screens for gardens. Some of the other products of my days in the woods were bavins, a light form of small wood in bundles for bread ovens. A heavier form, known as a frame faggot, was pressed flat and much favoured by town bakers. The round faggot was used by householders. Pea-sticks and bean-rods were sold by the bundle. Longer and smaller rods were tied seventy-five in a bundle and sent to the potteries of the Midlands and made into crates. Hazel wood in short lengths was used as legs and rungs, after shaping, in the making of Windsor chairs. Black dogwood or cornus was used in the making of gunpowder, and short lengths of hazel were used in the thatching of cottages, ricks and barns.

This was the work and activity which took the villagers into the woods. Hoops were made in Braishfield itself. What was the village shop of those days had a large garden and they were made at the top part of it,

Caleb Abraham, keeper of the village shop and bakery in The Square.

as they were at Dummers entering towards Pucknall and in a corner quite near to the rectory. A man named Charles Cooper was largely connected with the industry. In later years Caleb Abraham succeeded him. Of the various occupations I have been engaged in, work in the woods was my favourite.

And so it continued until January 1915 when I joined the 1st Hants Royal Garrison Artillery. Later we were the 154th Heavy Battery – a very smart and efficient crowd. The Battery consisted of two sections, or four sub-sections (A, B, C, and D), four guns from the Boer War, four gun teams – eight horses to a team, wagons and team drivers and gun crews. I joined as a gunner later to become a driver.

July of 1917 was a very wet and cold month and we were given a rum issue each night. One day one of our drivers said to me, "There is someone in Dickiebush who is known to you." Our wagon lines were at La Clytte, only a short distance away. One evening he came to see me and it was Charlie Abraham from Braishfield, who lived near us, was one of our choirboys and, like myself, a hoop-maker. In our conversation he told me his Regiment, the 15th Hants, were going to Italy. I replied that we were also hoping to go and get a change from the Ypres Salient. That was not to be. I showed Nobby, as we knew him, my pair of horses.

He said, "I can hardly imagine you linked up with a pair of horses." I replied, "I am very fond of them. One of them likes to shake hands." I heard no more of Nobby or the 15th. I think they suffered badly in the retreat of 1918. But I saw later Nobby's resting place, and his name on the cross marking it, in a small cemetery at Bihucourt.

In November 1918 I was on leave at the time of the Armistice with Bill, my brother, and I well remember the Service of Thanksgiving in Braishfield Church in the evening. The Reverend Chamney in his address said, "There are two amongst us who will be going back again. Let us be thankful that, for them and for many others, at least the guns are silent and the destruction has ceased." We returned and in late December Bill was one of the first to be demobbed. I stayed until late February 1919.

Coming home I found hoopmaking was all but finished and I obtained employment in Stanbridge Earls gardens where a staff of eight were employed. I was very interested and stayed almost three years when I left to go on the railway's permanent way, partly owing to a larger wage and partly to get cheaper journeys to see a certain young lady I was interested in who later became my wife.

Work on the permanent way was general maintenance of the track and of the fastenings, and grass cutting on the banks. Weeding the tracks in later years was done by spraying weedkiller from an engine and coaches adapted for the purpose. An annual job was to loosen all plates, connecting the ends of two rails together and giving a coat of oil and grease to hinder rail creep and rail buckling during hot weather. On occasions you were required to assist other gangs in the re-laying of a stretch of track. In the country districts four men were responsible for the maintenance of two miles of track.

Some winter duties like fog signalling were not so good, especially at night. You sat in a very small hut, similar to a sentry post, showing a green light from your fog lamp if the signal was clear. If it was at danger you gave a red light and the detonator you had fixed to one rail was exploded by the train as it passed and the driver then proceeded with caution to the next signal. My duty expired at 2am with the passing of the 'down' mail. Snow duties were hard, especially if you had a station or junction, and the particular section I was on had both. It was difficult to keep the points clear of snow and ice. We used rough salt which made them very rusty and they needed quite an amount of oil and cleaning to get them normal again.

One thing I must make mention of occurred in World War II. Owing to the threatened invasion of Jerry tanks, concrete blocks with slots to take bent and shaped rails were inserted at intervals in the permanent way which would, when fixed, create a blockade. They were erected monthly and a report sent to Eastleigh as to correct fitting. As some of us were members of the Railway Home Guard, we were requested to work with our rifles not far away from us. Every Friday we were to work at least for one hour with our respirators on. Later, land was purchased at Kimbridge and two new sidings were laid and a signal box built at one end for the use of extra traffic. One morning a section of Royal Engineers arrived and blew up both 'up' and 'down' running roads leaving buckled and twisted rails and a shell hole as large in size as those of the battlefields of World War I. It was done as a test, and there were almost as many top officials as workmen. After filling in the shell hole with stone, we laid sleepers and rails putting them back in order for running on again.

On reaching the age of sixty-five I retired from the railway and my colleagues presented me with a barometer which I still have. I did not retire from work but took employment with Hilliers Nurseries. Work there was autumn to spring, largely lifting plants, shrubs and smaller trees and packing to send by lorry and rail. Spring was for planting. Hoeing and weeding followed. One job I assisted with and was

The music books of the Braishfield Band.

greatly interested in was the lifting and moving of very big trees. A year or so before they may be wanted, a trench was dug a fair way out and many of the larger roots were cut off to encourage growth of the more smaller and fibrous ones. A year or so later you opened the trench again and dug under until you were able to raise it from its bed. Bags, stitched to form a covering, were rolled under one side. The tree was rolled back, the covering pulled through and sewn very tightly together making a nice ball of soil about six or seven feet across. Then the branches were tied in and it would be ready for transport. At the age of eighty-two, following an illness, I decided to retire, but continued my verger's duties at Braishfield Church until I was ninety-two and where I am now Honorary Verger. I am able still to do a little gardening.

The Braishfield Brass Band – 1907 to 1913

According to my grandfather the band started at the lower chapel in Newport Lane as a fife and drum band known as the Braishfield Temperance Band. Some while later it changed to brass and became the Braishfield Brass Band. They used to practise in a thatched shed just in front of the Newport Inn. They moved to a room belonging to Mr James Grace near the Dog and Crook and in my time to the Church Room. There were about fourteen or fifteen members. Yes, we wore uniform, blue with dark red facings and a stripe on the trouser legs which looked rather smart. My first bandmaster was W Thorpe and some of the members were: J Pottle and two sons, Silas Coster and brother, A Case, G Dummer and two sons, W and P Old, L Abraham, F Abraham, L Scorey and son. W Thorpe left us and went to a colliery band in Wales and E Baker became bandmaster. He was for some years organist at Nursling Church. Following him was Mr Tom Parsons, George's father. And last of all was Fred Pottle.

The Monday following Trinity Sunday was a great day for Braishfield, the day of the Band of Hope Temperance Fete, when with the band the village was paraded and various places called at, later returning for tea. In the evening the band played for dancing; the dances at that time were polka, waltz, lancers and quadrilles. This fete was held in a small field loaned by George Saunders who was living near where the War Memorial is now. The round-a-bouts were small and worked by a black pony walking round. Later it moved to the field

BRAISHFIELD BRASS BAND 1927

The Braishfield Brass Band in 1927 at the entrance to Newport Lane. The Terrace where Hedley Webb and Sid Scorey lived is on the right. In the background is The Lichens and, to the left, the Travis family's carpentry workshop where the coffins were made. Back row: far left – Fred Abraham. Front row: first from left – ? Goodridge, second from left – Hedley Webb. Other known names: Fred Pottle (leader), Jess Wells, Perce Old, George Dummer, Bill Dummer, Bill Gritt with drum.

where the bungalows are near the chapel and modern round-a-bouts and swing boats driven by an engine were engaged. It had a very good organ for the latest popular songs.

Three local villages, Michelmersh, Ampfield and Hursley, held an annual Friendly Society Fete. At each there was a church parade on a Sunday, parades through the village on a weekday, the annual dinner with loyal toasts and speeches (taking rather a long time), then later playing for dancing in the evening. Round-a-bouts and Fun of the Fair were in attendance. Those events made up a great part of village holidays. Another engagement was the annual flower show, started between the wars, where it was playing a march or two and selections. There was dancing in the evening but no round-a-bouts.

We played at the Church Sunday School Treat held at Jermyns House, the home of Mr and Mrs Pepper. The children were conveyed in farm wagons from the village.

On Christmas Day in the afternoon the band assembled and visited the Manor, the Lodge and Braishfield

House. On Boxing Day the tour would start around 9am with the walk to Ampfield calling first at Ampfield House, then the White Horse, the Vicarage and Rat Lake Farm. Our first call in Hursley was North End House, then the two inns and one or two large houses. After a brief rest we moved to Park House where, after playing several tunes, we were given the invitation to see the large Christmas tree standing in the hall, awaiting the arrival later of children from Farley, Hursley and Braishfield in a number of farm wagons. It was a treat from Sir George and Lady Cooper. After viewing the tree and its many presents, we received the invitation to go to the back, give an item or two and then go inside for refreshments.

First we played a march, then a dance, maybe a polka or waltz, barn dance or schottische which were popular dances of those days. From there we made our way home via Slackstead and Pucknall. We were out again for a short while in the evening. We gave the village a good opportunity to listen to their band.

One evening to be remembered was our visit to Farley and Slackstead near the end of the Christmas festival. First call was to Farley Rectory, then to a cottage which stood at the bottom of the drive. Walter Brown lived there. After waking him up to our presence by playing a good stirring march, we were all given a welcome in and a good part of an evening followed. Songs were sung,

The band playing at the flower show in the mid-1930s. The marquee was set up in the field south of the chapel where the houses in Hill View Road now stand. Bill Gritt is playing the bass drum.

as practically each bandsman had a song. Parts of them I remember still. One was, 'If those lips could only speak'. We then went along to the keepers cottage in the lane going toward Slackstead. William Bark lived there and again, after a march, invited us in. As we were enjoying the evening, Mr Bark was busy with a stew pan on the kitchen range pouring in several ingredients and stirring them until he was satisfied it was ready to pour out. I did not partake, but I imagine it was very strong. After another song or two we left for home, and that was about the end of our Christmas tour.

Later followed the band supper. It was first given by Mr and Mrs De Clermont of Braishfield Lodge, and when they left, kindly taken over by Mr and Mrs Griffiths of Woolley Green. This was the way of it. We arrived at 7pm. At the front of the house we first played a march and several more items. Mr and Mrs Griffiths would come out, give us a welcome and say, "Will you give the girls (meaning the servants) an item or two." We usually gave them a good lively march and a couple of dances. We would go inside and Mr and Mrs Griffiths would join us. We usually left for home after a very enjoyable evening of singing and dancing about 10.30 or 11pm. On the departure of Mr and Mrs Griffiths, Mr Ashley Dodd became our host.

1913 was our last visit as in 1914 we were at war. On our tour of Christmas 1913 there seemed to be a very popular march and many people asked us for it. The name was 'Under the Double Eagle'. It was a good one but I believe it was of German origin. My last appearance with the band was late October 1913 when Mr Ashley Dodd entertained the children of Farley and Braishfield schools to a tea and fete in a field opposite the lane to Farley. It was on a large scale with a fun fair and all its attractions, our band and a marvellous spread. It was great.

I did not rejoin the band after the war but I must pay this tribute to the village band for its services to the Armistice Day church service. The first, as far as I remember, was in 1919. The band attended and played the first hymn followed by the service. Then came the procession, led by the cross and followed by the choir, band and congregation. It went by the back way through the village, the band playing as they marched. There was a short service at the War Memorial and finally a hymn from the band, usually 'Abide with me'. A number of ex-servicemen were inspected, and it was also the band's annual service. With the coming of World War II the service was discontinued until the war ended. By that time the band had broken up.

These memories were written over a period of years, the final one in 1985.

Born and brought up in the village Sid Scorey and his wife, Sis, lived at The Firs in Jermyn Lane for all their married life. For his last few years he lived with his niece, Pat, in Chandlers' Ford. He died in 1989 aged ninety-seven.

The Braishfield Band marching through Romsey from the Market Place in 1938. Henry Dewey, centre, is playing the trombone.

The Bowns of Braishfield
Tony Stares

1880s–1950s

The Bown family came to Braishfield early in the nineteenth century and set up business as agricultural engineers at Brook House. My grandfather, James Higgins Bown, was a wheelwright by trade but his first job, aged nine in 1875, was to walk ahead of a traction engine carrying a red flag. On his marriage he moved to the Dog and Crook where his wife's parents were the proprietors at the end of the nineteenth century. During this time he worked as a wheelwright at Strong's yard in Romsey.

My mother, Dorothy, was born at the Dog and Crook in 1896 and when she was nine years old the family moved to Laurel Cottage in Lower Street. She remembered as a child seeing a man breaking stones for the roads at the road junction nearby. They had a front garden with an apple tree in the middle of the lawn. By the side of the house and at the back were pig sties and stretching along the rear of the property were fruit trees and chicken runs; the vegetable garden was on the other side of the house. Water was drawn from a well by hand pump in the kitchen. Tap water at the sink was drawn from a rainwater tank at the side of the house.

James Bown (right) and a colleague by a newly made wagon on the Hursley Estate Home Farm around 1910.

My mother and grandmother walked to and fro to Romsey to shop and at other times rode in a governess cart. They used to have musical evenings with friends and relations. When my mother was in her teens she had a bicycle on which she used to go to work as a dressmaker, and she went cycling with girl friends from Braishfield. My grandfather had a brick building by the side of the cottage which he called 'the shop' where he did his carpentry, working at the same time for various employers including the Hursley Estate and Mr King at the Manor. He was for some time a parish councillor with a particular interest in footpaths.

He lived at Laurel Cottage until his death in 1954, aged eighty-eight, my grandmother having died in 1928.

Between the world wars there was a baker in Braishfield, Mr Abraham. He had a large van and I remember the cottage loaves delivered by him to the Corn Market in Romsey.

During and after the Second World War our butcher's shop, Stares, delivered in Braishfield on Wednesdays and Saturdays.

As children before and during the Second World War my sister and

The Dog and Crook in 1901. Tony's mother, Dorothy as a little girl, is on the far right with her parents, James and Mary Bown, tenants of the pub. The sign on the wall reads 'Strong's Romsey Ales'. The group of customers have arrived by various means, including horse, bicycle and Shanks' pony. Some, with scythes, appear to have come straight from the fields.

I used to take our ponies from the stables in Mill Lane, Romsey, to Mr Cobbold, the farrier, in Lower Street.

Tony's father, Walter Stares, ran the pork butcher's shop in the Cornmarket, Romsey, which he had taken over from his grandfather, Alfred, on his return from the First World War. Walter Stares married Dorothy Bown at All Saints' Braishfield in 1924. The couple made their home in the Cornmarket and Tony and his sister, Audrey, were born 'over the shop'. The children kept their ponies stabled in Mill Lane and would ride them out to Mr Cobbold in Braishfield for shoeing. Tony followed his father into the business and retired after forty-three years at Christmas 1991. He and his wife, Heather, now live in Awbridge.

James and Mary Bown and visitors outside Laurel Cottage in Paynes Hay Lane in the summer of 1928.

2:30 at the War Memorial
Doug Stewart

1979–1980s

Douglas Stewart, aged nineteen, returning from his sponsored bicycle ride to Scotland in aid of the Village Hall Building Fund. He cycled one thousand three hundred and eighty-nine miles in less than a month in August 1979.

Sometimes when I shut my eyes I am there. It's a Sunday afternoon; the sun is high in the sky and from all directions friends are sauntering to the War Memorial.

It became a ritual for a generation of young people. Even during the more fraught moments of exam revision, there was always 2:30 at the War Memorial.

It sounds so tame now, in a world of Pokemon and cyberspace, but we all looked forward to Sunday afternoons: to long walks through meandering wildflower lined footpaths, and the longer excursions to Farley Mount; sometimes even further afield, as we discovered the simple joys of youth hostelling in Wales.

It was our mission to protect the footpaths, to ensure they were walked and cared for. This was a time when concern for the environment was at its height and we worried that footpaths, unused and unloved, would soon be ploughed over and lost.

The Guinness Race, the ultimate walk of all, took place once a year to mark the end of the Christmas activities which involved three nights of carol singing under the leadership of Sarah Boothman. It celebrated

The Guinness Race walkers at Farley Mount in 1983. Left to right: James Stonham, Caroline Stonham (nee Trueman), ?, Douglas Stewart, Linda Fielder, Rury Freckleton, Fiona Freckleton, Timothy Wilson, ?, Hannah Boothman.

our love for Guinness, the great outdoors, friends and the perfection of the Hampshire countryside.

Sometimes, when I shut my eyes, I am there with the most special friends I ever made and the countryside we all bonded with. Braishfield is a truly special place.

Douglas was born in 1959 in Dundee and moved to the village with his parents in 1964. His early interest in gardening was fostered by work experience at two local nurseries and he embarked on a career in horticulture becoming head of that department at Bishop Burton College in Yorkshire. Now their Marketing Manager he travels and lectures extensively and is a regular contributor to Radio Humberside's weekly gardening programme, 'The Great Outdoors'.

The Braishfield Seven
Margaret Stewart

1960s–1980s

Nearly forty years ago when I first arrived in Braishfield there were a group of village ladies who called themselves The Braishfield Seven. Their main aim was to raise funds for many charities both in and out of the village. This was accomplished by putting together variety concerts in which they all took part.

These concerts were staged in the old WI Hut which was, at that time, on ground opposite April Cottage. The hall at concert time was absolutey packed. One had to be there early or it was standing room only (I dread to think of the fire hazard!) The hilarious sketches, songs and dance routines are too numerous to mention.

In view of the sad passing of Margaret Old I feel I must mention one act which involved two of the 'Seven' in particular, Margaret Old and Joan Parsons.

The Braishfield Seven's last show in the WI Hall in 1981 in a revue called 'The Tramps'. Left to right: Joan Parsons, Rita Stitt, Shirley Smith, Girlie Old, Edna Cottle, Janet Cook.

Right: Moving scenery for a Braishfield Seven show. Girlie Old is outside the Newport with Mr Owen's horse and cart.

Far right: Joan Parsons as an old fashioned bathing beauty in one of the Braishfield Seven's revues. Joan had to buy a fresh herring every night. "The cat did very well!"

A sort of boat was constructed in which Margaret and Joan sat at one side of the stage. Margaret wore a striped blazer and a straw boater whilst Joan wore elegant clothes and had a parasol in her hand. To the tune of 'Cruising Down The River' the boat was pulled by Joan's husband Bill and, I think, Stan Parsons (unseen) until it reached the other side of the stage with Margaret rowing across.

It was so funny; we all looked forward to the variety shows.

Happy memories!

Margaret and Jim Stewart and their son, Douglas, came to Braishfield from Banff in Scotland in 1964 when Jim took up an appointment with Ordnance Survey in Southampton. As a family they made a marked contribution to the life of the village. Now a widow, Margaret has recently moved to Romsey.

Events

1935–2000

The Jubilee Day procession in Braishfield Road in 1935 to celebrate the Silver Jubilee of the Coronation of King George V and Queen Mary. The lime trees bordering the recreation ground were planted by the school children to mark this event. Peggy (Alford) Woodley and Joyce (Old) Alford have vivid memories of digging holes for the saplings, with three children to each tree. The lime trees, mature specimens now, are a prominent feature and give welcome shade to the activities on the recreation ground. Known faces: Bert Cawte, Peggy Cawte, Margery Old, Rosemary Dunning, Milly Parsons, Maggie Moody.

The Newport versus The Club (The Social Club) Boxing Day football match in 1952. The participants and spectators are marching to the match along Braishfield Road past the chapel (on the left of the picture) led by Boxer Old's goat! Left to right: Edna Cottle, Rita Stitt, Janet Cottle (Cook), Boxer Old playing his 'oompah', Tom Brady, Ted Glister, Ron Gritt with the banner reading 'Gales for Goals', Bessie Old with the goat, Girlie Old, Shirley Cottle (Smith). The other banner reads 'Up the Clubites'.

Above left:
The opening party at the village hall in 1982.

Above right
Coronation Day Carnival 2nd June 1953. Ken Vear (seated) as Carnival Queen with attendants Frank Marshallsay (left), 'Chippy' Babey and Hilda Vear.

Right:
Retirement party for Mr C H E 'Bardy' Bardell, organist at All Saints' Church for over twenty-five years, taken in the church porch in 1982. Left to right: Back row: Lucy Freckleton, Elizabeth Harris, Linda Fielder, Sidney Scorey, Sarah Boothman, Nick Shepherd. Middle row: Ruth Fielder, Mr Bardell, Daniel Richards, Hannah Boothman. Front row: Kate Quarendon, Rebecca Freckleton, Elizabeth Fielder, Clare Chisholm.

Top:
The annual Braishfield Seven fête at Elm Grove in the 1960s. Teas were served on the verandah and all the stalls and sideshows were set up in the garden. Ice creams were sold from the summerhouse. Everyone waited outside behind the tape until the fete was declared open. No buying beforehand! The group raised considerable funds for various charities with their very popular concerts. The contestants in the children's fancy dress competition are pictured here.

Middle:
Before the outing. The Romsey Over Sixties Club, popular with Braishfield pensioners, is gathered outside the Crosfield Hall in Romsey in the 1960s. After the new village hall was built Walter Trueman started a Braishfield club which flourished during the 1980s and 1990s. Left to right: Elsie Barnes, Ethel Dunford, Mrs Cook, Bertha Old, Mrs Still (partly hidden), Mrs Randall, ?, ?, Ruth Alford, Bob Russell, ?.

Bottom:
The annual Social Club Boxing Day football match in 1965 or 1966, the men in night-dresses versus the ladies in pyjamas.

Top:
A tug-of-war in costume between the Social Club and one of the pubs at the flower show on the recreation ground in the mid-1980s. The Social Club team: Front to back: Janet Blake, Marion Pace, Ruth Fielder, Joan Glister, Mandy Payne, Sheena Gillingham, Delia Pritchard, Maggie Batchelor. Known faces among the spectators: Lisa Sillence, Don Greenyer (the steward of The Club), Ruby White, Alan Light, Dorothy Balson, Ida Coffin, Joanne Light, Paul Fowgies, Eileen Stickley, Mike Stickley, Nick Shepherd. Jack Batchelor is on the left, crouching, with his back to the camera.

Bottom:
The United Reformed Church Christmas Nativity play in December 1985. Left to right: Back row: David Anstey, Richard Light, Stewart McMaster, Kevin Light, Mark Anstey, Christopher Hackman, Joanne Milsom, Victoria Snellgrove, David Irish, Vicky Hackman. Middle row: Lee McMaster, David Fildie, Matthew Payne. Front row: Emma Snellgrove, Richard Milsom, Allan Holyoake, Colin Holyoake, Laura Snellgrove, Adam Fildie, James Light, Joanne Light.

Top:
A gathering of supporters from Braishfield following the ordination of Tim Wilson as a priest at Hereford Cathedral in June 1990. Tim was organist and choirmaster at All Saints' Church and was much involved in youth work. He directed a number of musical productions in the new village hall. Left to right: Jill Wilson (Tim's mother), Bruce Kington, Rector of All Saints' since 1981, Lucy Kington, Meryl Balchin, Elizabeth Fielder, Nick Shepherd, Daniel Kington, Luke Kington, Ruth Fielder, James Kington, Tim Wilson, Kate Quarendon, Wendy Quarendon, Grenville Richards, Mollie Russell, Rosalie Gurr, Sonia Gurr, Gemma Fiddes, Sandy Richards, Sarah Boothman, Norman Wilson (Tim's father).

Bottom:
The village picnic and concert to celebrate the millennium in June 2000 on the recreation ground. The mature lime trees, planted in 1935, can be seen in the background.

Rita and Girlie
Rita Stitt (1926–1998) &
Margaret Old (1922–1999)

1927–1941

Girlie and Rita at the door of April Cottage on the fiftieth anniversary of VE Day, 8th May 1995. With them is Rita's daughter, Elizabeth, and the dogs, Jaffa and Biddy.

In June 1995 Braishfield School invited Margaret Old and Rita Stitt to talk to the children about their schooldays and memories. The following is edited from a transcript of this encounter.

We went to school when we were five and we stayed a long time until we were fourteen. When Margaret started school there was a bell in the belfry. "I thought, 'Shan't I be glad to get up in that other room so I can pull the bell', but before I got there the belfry wasn't safe. The bell used to be rung two or three times a day, you could see it from outside as well. It was a huge bell. It went to Hoddinott's farm at Elm Grove."

The netball teams in 1936, the over-fourteens play the under-fourteens. Captain Allen, a school governor who lived at Battledean (now Newport House), lends his support. Left to right: Ena Dewey, Peggy Cawte, Margaret Old, Joan Pinhorn, Dorrie Fielding, Doris Dewey, May Emily Rogers (teacher), Joyce Old, Sylvia Cook, Cynthia Fielder, Eileen Byford, Joy Logan, Marjory Old. May Emily (Maisie) Rogers married Fred Benham in 1938.

Mrs Dane (left) and Miss Dorothy Bacon. "At that time Mrs Dane was the governess, the headteacher."

We had no electric lights at all, no water, no taps, no school lunches and everyone had to go home at dinner time. Some children had quite a long way to walk and only those that lived three miles away were allowed to bring food. We had three teachers and there were about seventy-five children. One of our teachers is still alive, she must be in her nineties. Her name was Miss Euston and she lived at Ampfield. The other teachers all lived in the village. In the evening we used to come back to the recreation ground and practice netball. The boys played football, and we played another game called stoolball*. The teachers came out as well because they lived in the village. We used to do a lot of practice so that hopefully we could beat some of the other schools we played against like Michelmersh and Ampfield.

Mrs May Emily Benham came when she was eighteen and she's still got a very special place in our hearts because she was a wonderful teacher, kind and helpful. She came at eighteen and she stayed all her life. She used to give up all her time for us. At that time Mrs Dane was the governess, the head teacher.

The only heating we had was an open fire in each classroom with just a few lumps of coal on and it used to be bitterly cold in winter. The draught used to come up through the floorboards. We still had to have windows open because in those days they thought that lots of fresh air was good for us. "You've no need to put your jackets on. Run about when you get outside". We used to run round the boys' playground when it was frosty, and when we came in we had to write a composition. We beat our hands against our arms to warm them up because it was so cold.

* stoolball – an ancient Sussex game, the first reference to it was written in the fifteenth century. Milking stools were used by the maids as wicket and, the legs having been removed, bat. The game survives, played by women and girls in the main, in its home county. The foot square, head height wooden targets, standing on four legs, are set sixteen yards apart. With two batsmen, a small ball and much the same rules as our summer game it is often described as 'cricket in the air'.

We were never allowed a fountain pen. We wrote with old, scratchy pens and we hated the new nibs which were even worse. And we had ink. Every Monday the monitor mixed up the ink powder in a big enamel jug with a spout on it and went round filling the ink wells every day.

We didn't have anything on the floor and we had desks – rows and rows of desks. There was a little ledge where the headteacher kept her cane and we were quite worried when we saw her hand go up to get it out. Girls got the cane as well as boys. We used to be quite mischievous and naughty sometimes. There was a punishment book. If you got the cane it was over and done with, but if you got your name in the punishment book it was awful because it was there for always.

We weren't allowed to talk in class at all so it was all very quiet and you were taught from a blackboard at the front of the class. When we weren't doing our compositions or dictation or arithmetic sometimes we would have an order, "Arms folded", and sometimes it used to be, "Hands behind your back", and we sat like that to listen to history or geography lessons. Sometimes Margaret would talk in class and so she used to stay in either at playtime or after school and write on double sheets of arithmetic foolscap, "I must not talk in class". It made us very late going home so we would rather do it at playtime than after school because if we were late home our parents asked, "Why are you late today?" and then we used to have to say that we had been kept in and what for and we got punished again at home.

Braishfield School assembled on Empire Day in 1933. Known faces: Bill Parsons, Girlie Old, Rita Stitt, Peggy Cawte.

PT demonstration on the recreation ground in 1938/39. The school and schoolhouse are in the background.

A dentist came to the school. He used to pull out our teeth in the Infants' Room and he came with these awful looking drills and things, and he filled our teeth and pulled them out at school. You couldn't go home afterwards. You had to go on with your work even if you had two or three teeth out. The doctor came as well, and the nurse used to look in our hair to see if it was clean.

Margaret had long plaits, nearly long enough to sit on, and Rita would catch hold of a plait and pull just as if it was a cow's tail. Sometimes she found herself tied to her chair with those plaits by the naughty boy behind and when she would go to get up she couldn't.

We belonged then to the British Empire, so every May we had Empire Day at school and it was wonderful. Flags went out and we had all sorts of patriotic things going on in the playground. We had a half-day holiday afterwards. We used to have another very special day called 'pound day' when each child, if they could, brought a pound of something to school; a pound of sugar or cheese, rice or tapioca, and it was collected and taken down to Romsey Hospital. They were very pleased with that.

When the school door was opened for us to go home we all rushed out. The whole village could hear when school had finished because we used to do dreadful shouting and made a lot of noise once we were let out. We'd had to be so quiet in school.

The oak tree outside the school was put in by our Uncle Walt. We all had to plant the lime trees in the recreation ground for the Silver Jubilee of King George V and Queen Mary in 1935. Mrs Dane and Mrs

Benham planted the copper beech just outside the gate at the back of the recreation ground.

We used to have seasons of games. We had skipping in the springtime and conkers in the autumn. We skipped to rhymes, rolled hoops along and had games of marbles. We played hopscotch in the road on Saturday mornings and holidays. There was no traffic about and even if a car came along you had masses of time to get out of the way because you could hear it coming. They were very noisy. Once a year my father hired a car, one of those lovely old cars with running boards and all leather seats. One day we would go to the seaside. We would tell our friends that we were going so they would all get alongside the road to see us in the car and we waved and we thought we were pretty special, like the Queen, and it was great fun. There were about three cars in the village then. Mr Dane, the governess's husband had one, Mrs King at the Manor had a car and Admiral and Lady Bacon, and that was about it. If you wanted to go to somewhere like Romsey you had to walk or bicycle, because there was one village bus that only went once a week.

Mrs King who lived at Braishfield Manor used to take an interest in the school and she ran the Band of Mercy. We all belonged to it and made this promise, "I promise to be kind to all animals and to do all in my power to protect them from all harm". It was probably a country-wide thing like the RSPCA. We used to get newsletters and things and were made very aware of animals and all their sufferings. She was very kind in that way. Every

Percival Old, Rita's father, in chauffeur's uniform at the wheel of the Braishfield House automobile taken inside the gate of Braishfield House. The lady passenger on the right is probably Miss Eaton. The photograph, taken around 1920, was made into a postcard and sent by Percival to his sister, Lily, who was working at Greatbridge House near Romsey. His message reads, "Dear Lil, Just a card to let you know I am still alive. Hope you are well and I hope you will like this card. I don't think it's half bad. Love & XXX from Perce".

Three Girl Guides: Rita, Doreen Dunford and Rosie Dunning.

We belonged to the Brownies, and met at the Church Room. It used to be called the Parish Room. The uniform was quite different to what it is now but we still had a toadstool and made our promises. Then we belonged to the Girl Guides. My old captain used to say the Braishfield girls were wonderful. When the Boy Scouts came out of their meeting at their hut close by we chanted at them, "Boy Sprouts, Boy Sprouts, look your shirts are hanging out". So you see we were quite mischievous really. We told our guide captain when we saw her a little while ago and she said, "I don't believe that!" So we weren't really quite as good as she thought we were.

Christmas she used to give us the most wonderful Christmas party. We used to collect at the War Memorial and then walk up in a crocodile to Braishfield Manor. There was a hut up there where we had this wonderful party. There was a conjurer and presents and that was really one of the highlights of our year because we didn't have many parties.

During the war we had lots of evacuee children so they made the school into a girls' school and the old village hall was the boys' school,

When evacuee children came to the village the school was split. The boys were taught at the WI Hall and the girls had their classes at the school. Pictured here outside the hall in 1942 are: Left to right: Back row: Roy Bottomley*, John Webb, Jim Glister, Horace Darby, Maurice Freegard, Eric Freegard, Arthur Sweet, Dennis Shannon*, ?, Ted Glister, Peter Drake, Ron Gritt, ?, Philip Bonney*. Front row: Victor Hunt, Richard Sealy*, Roy Shannon.

*evacuee

209

The Old Village Stores at the turn of the century. Fred Abraham, in an apron with a bread basket over his shoulder, is standing in front of their horse and cart. His father, Caleb, is by the door. The shop front can be seen on the extreme right. The bakery, which was separate from the cottage, has long been demolished.

so we were split up and we weren't a mixed school any more. They brought their own teacher with them, a master called Mr Metherill, and that was something quite new for us as we had only had a governess. We were all issued with gas masks then and we carried them to school with us.

When Margaret left school she went to work at Braishfield House as a parlour maid. "I didn't like the job and, to tell the truth, I was really glad when the war came. I thought that I could really do something now. I went and joined the land army and got a job in the village which was lucky. Mr Owen, the farmer, was a school governor and Chairman of the Milk Marketing Board. I went to work at Elm Grove. I started at six o'clock in the morning. We used to hand milk cows, it took me quite a little while to learn how to do it. I remember very often getting up when a cow was going to calve. The farmer was ill at the time and I went down to the farm to see if the cow was all right. Then I stayed until she had calved. Then it was back home to bed for an hour and up again at six o'clock in the morning and away to milk."

At the house now called The Old Village Stores there was a shop and a bakery and we would work there on Saturdays. When Margaret was about twelve she started serving in the shop. "It was nine o'clock in the morning and I finished at half past two in the afternoon. I went home with ninepence, which I was very much pleased with. Mr Abraham was the baker. Before I went to school, when I was very little, I often used to go in the bakehouse and see them get the oven ready and put the bread in. First they put the packets, the bundles of wood, in the oven to heat it up, and when it was hot they swabbed all the ashes out. They had all the bread ready to go in the oven on great long peels and they put it in, and when it was cooked they drew it out of the oven. It was lovely, crusty bread and it smelled beautiful. I haven't tasted any like it since.

"Mr Abraham had a horse and van and he sometimes took me with him delivering round the village. He used to ask me if I wanted to drive Ginger. He was a beautiful horse. He'd know just where to stop at people's houses, I didn't have to say, 'Whoa', or anything.

"I also went with him when he delivered bread into Romsey with Ginger and the van. On the way home he would call into the doctor's surgery for any medicine to come back to Braishfield. He went to the International Stores to see if there were groceries for anyone in the village and on to the railway station for any deliveries for Braishfield. By the time Mr Abraham got back from delivering he had to make a start at his bakehouse on the bread for the next day. This stage was called 'setting the sponge' and he made it at ten o'clock at night.

"I got home one lunchtime from school and my mother said – 'Do you know what – they've had to have poor Ginger put to sleep.' I was very upset, he was a great friend."

Most houses had a well or shared one. At April Cottage we just had a spring

Bessie Cawte, Dorcas Gritt and Madge Old at the water pump in Hill View Road in 1937.

Emma Old at the back door of Fairbourne Place in the late 1930s where she was frequently visited by her extended family, many of whom lived in the village. She lived there until her death in 1939 where her daughter, Lily Proom and her family, cared for her.

at the top of the garden, and about six people from the cottages around went there for water and carted it down in buckets. It is still running down the ditch in our garden.

Everyone kept a pig, and we had chickens in the garden. Rita's grandfather kept pigs. "One day, when they were born, there was a very tiny pig, a runt, a lot smaller than all the others so he told my aunt that she could take care of it. The pig became a pet. It was very friendly and tame and she pushed it about in her doll's pram, and when she came home from school it went to meet her. As they do, it grew into a very big pig, so her father said that it had to go and one day the pig went to market and my aunt became quite ill. She was so heartbroken because the pig had gone. They had to get the doctor to her and thought she had gone into a decline and was going to die because she missed the pig so much. She's still alive now at nearly a hundred and she still talks about her pig!"

Sundays were very busy because we sang in the church choir and went to Sunday School. Our grandmother lived down at the other end of the village. We visited her on Sundays and had great fun down at Granny's with all our cousins. The family all lived in the village so if Mother wasn't home you just went to one of the aunts or cousins. It was great for continuity.

Years ago people used to be poor and they didn't have very much and so when a new baby arrived into a family it used to be really quite difficult. Up at the rectory they kept what they called 'the baby box' which had everything in it for a newborn baby; blankets, nightdresses for the mother, and baby clothes. When a baby was going to arrive the baby box went to the house and they kept it for about six weeks before it was returned to the rectory ready for the next baby. Milk and food was delivered every day from the rectory when the mother was in bed with the baby or if anyone was ill.

We never locked our doors at home; people just didn't have to lock up because there weren't burglars about in the village. Everybody felt very safe. We could go anywhere. The farmers used to let us run all over their fields. We spent all our summer holidays on the farms, and we loved the farming year. We helped with the haymaking and the harvest time. We rode home on the horses, about three of us on each horse, plodding along the country lanes back to the farm.

We played and made camps down in the chalk pits and there were thick overhanging branches; we called them fire escapes, and we were able to swing from one side of the pit to the other. We used to get into one pit, picking up bits of wood to take home for the fire, and you would hear someone go, "Hrrumph, hrrumph". That was the farmer coming along, and we ran then because we were afraid of him. He was a very good farmer but he didn't like children trespassing. But generally we could go anywhere. We really didn't have very many toys, not a lot to play with. We had to make our own. The boys knocked up old trolleys, and we were able to go around on those.

We used to have gangs. Rita was once very keen to belong to one gang and asked to join. They said, "You have got to do the initiation to get into our gang. Meet us tonight, up over Aubreys". This was a footpath going over the fields. There was some old carthorse sheds and they said, "You've got to jump from the roof of the shed right down into this manger place, full of straw". She didn't think she was brave enough to do it, but she so wanted to join that she jumped and made it, so it was really worth it in the end.

And we played games like cricket. We only had old bits of wood for wickets but we did have a cricket bat because we saved up Oxo cube wrappers for it. We needed one hundred and sixty and it seemed we were eating Oxos forever. Rita's mother used to say, "What would you like before you go to bed?" We usually had cocoa, but her brother used to

Carthorses at Elm Grove Farm. "We rode home on the horses, about three of us on each horse, plodding along the country lanes back to the farm."

say, "Tell her you'll have Oxo. And tell her you'll have two tonight". We didn't like Oxo very much but because he was so keen to get this cricket bat we kept on having it. We didn't have the money to buy one so it was the only way, and eventually we saved enough. Rita's brother always wanted to be the captain and when we played in the evening she always had to do the fielding and never seemed to get into bat before they pulled the stumps up and it was time to go home. Eventually she refused to field anymore so he said, "Well, if you'll come and play tonight you can be Don Bradman". Now he was quite a famous cricketer, and she thought, "How wonderful. I'm to be Don Bradman for the night", and went out to play.

Rita's parents, Percival and Laura Old, in 1953, the last picture of them taken together.

Rita was born into the Old family in Braishfield and spent most of her life in the village. For many years she was Secretary of the Hursley Estate. An active member of All Saints' Church she taught in the Sunday School as well as supporting the United Reformed Church. She was especially loved by the children of the village. A founder member of the Braishfield Seven Concert Party she was also at various times a school governor, member of the Braishfield Parish Council and WI, and a founder member of the Braishfield Horticultural Society when it re-formed. Rita died in 1998 leaving a daughter, Elizabeth, and a son, Alan.

Margaret, generally known as Girlie, lived and worked all her life in the village. She was a parlour maid at Braishfield House with the Vincent family and then worked for many years at Elm Grove Farm for Mr Owen and subsequently for the Hoddinotts. She loved her work with the dairy herd and had a great fondness for carthorses, judging at the Romsey Show for many years. Later on she was gardener at Braishfield Manor for Mr and Mrs Gibbs. Girlie, like her cousin, Rita, was a founder member of the Braishfield Seven and an active member of All Saints' Church. She was show secretary of the annual village flower show. The garden at April Cottage where she and Rita lived was her pride and joy, and a delight to passers by. She died in 1999.

The Braishfield House Fire
June Thomson

late 1930s

A WI fete at Orchard Cottage in the early 1960s. Left to right: Babette Brown, George Brown, ?, George Spikins, Daisy Old, June bowling, Lily Proom, David Andrews, ?, Samuel Boothman, Mary Boothman.

I remember it was on my birthday in June, many years ago, that my family and I were woken from our sleep in the middle of the night by the sound of a succession of explosions. We were in those days living in one of the Pond Cottages. When we saw through the window that the sky was as bright as day my father, quickly left his bed and went outside to investigate. What he discovered was that Braishfield House was ablaze. He immediately returned, made us put on some clothes, and ushered us out into the garden. We watched as the building burned and the sparks flew into the air, many of which landed on our thatched roof. My sister and I were terrified. Our father decided to offer his services and left us together with our mother, in the care of the next door neighbour, Charlie Saunders, who tried to console us by giving us sweets which he normally only gave us at weekends.

In those times, the village was not blessed with a mains water supply and the fire brigade had to pump water from the nearby pond, which fortunately in those days always contained a plentiful supply of water. Whilst all this was going on the son of Mr Newby Vincent, the then

June's mother, Lily Proom, Braishfield's first female motor-cyclist, on her Royal Enfield in 1920.

owner, climbed a ladder to rescue his sister's small dog from a bedroom. Meanwhile, my father was given the task of guarding the bull, housed in a nearby pen, who was terrified, stamping his feet and roaring loudly. Father afterwards admitted that he, too, was scared.

We later learned that there had been a party at Braishfield House that evening. Some thought that perhaps a discarded cigarette was the cause of the fire, but we never knew. The explosions we were told were the result of shotgun cartridges being caught up in the fire. The house was burned to the ground – something I will never forget.

June, the daughter of Lily (Old) and Bertram Proom, was born and raised in the village. She lives in the family cottage with her husband, Bob.

3 and 4 Pond Cottages in the 1950s. June's family lived in the one on the right.

Index

Numbers in *italics* are illustrations; numbers in **bold** represent text and illustrations

Abbotswood Farm 162
accidents
   boy burnt 1
   cornfield fire 5
   farm fire 88
   gunpowder explosion 4
   horse and trap 120
   house collapse 87
   house fires 2, 78, 215-16
   lightning 3, 80
   meteors 80
   pub fire 21, 94, 104-6
   road 94
   squashed bucket 87
   woman killed by horse 15
agriculture *see* farms and farming
All Saints' Church ix, 8, **175**
   architecture **33**-4
   baby box 212-13
   baptisms 70
   centenary of consecration 33, *167*
   choir 88, *113*, *118*, 167
   church magazine cover *31*
   clock 3-4, *33*
   film location 117
   graveyard 71
   interior *32*
   ordination gathering *203*
   organ 70
   prayer book presentation to organist *70*
   retirement party for organist *200*
   Sunday school 131
   weddings *32*, 70, *85*

allotments 133
Amberley 47, 49
Ampfield 188
Ampfield House 50, 189
Ampfield Wood 126
animals and birds
   chickens 67, 88, 127, 160
   cows/dairy cattle 51-2, 72-4, *73*, 79, 81, 107, 148-50, *149*, 210
   deer 75
   dogs *78*, 99, *101*, 172
   donkeys 87, 167
   ducks 160, *161*
   ferrets 169
   geese 160
   goats 160
   heifer *57*
   kindness to 64, 91
   peahens 75-6
   pheasants 24
   pigs *24*, 54, 67, *78*, 88, 106-7, 133, 136, 160, **161**, 179, 182, 192, 212
   rabbits 54, 75, 160, 166, 169
   scruff dog racing 99
   sheep 2, 81-2
   snakes 170
   vermin 172
   see also bees; horses
Annie's Cottage *23*
April Cottage *204*
archaeological digs **109**, 157-9
army torch light display 4
austerity years 6-8, 30

babies 212-13
    Christening group *68*
    see also children
Band of Hope
    Fete 187-8
    magic lantern entertainment 37
Band of Mercy 64, 91, 208
Barneys *see* Romanies
Battledene House *86*
bees 161
birds *see* animals and birds
Blackthorn Close 11
Boares Garden 17, 92
Bowling Green Bungalow 62, 65
Bowling Green Cottage 62
Boy Scouts *see* Braishfield Boy Scouts
Braishfield
    civil parish status 32
    constituency boundaries 22
    history viii-ix
    population 9, 22
    village twinning **26-8**
Braishfield Boy Scouts 61, 209
    stocks *101*
Braishfield Brass Band 187-90, *188, 189, 191*
    see also Village Band
Braishfield Brownies *111*, 209
Braishfield Country Fair *see* Country Fair
Braishfield Cricket Club 32, **144-6**
Braishfield Cubs *112*
Braishfield Football Club 27, 32, **138-43**
Braishfield Garage 11
Braishfield Girl Guides 10, *87*, 130, **209**
Braishfield House 29, 188-9, 209
    fire 215-16
Braishfield Lodge *see* The Lodge
Braishfield Manor *see* The Manor

Braishfield Music and Drama Society (BMADS) *114*
Braishfield Road 2, *50*, 62
Braishfield School ix, 1, **35-46**, 63, 68, *84*, 127-8, 161, 181
    attendance 35-7, 40-1
    attendance certificate *42*
    caning 206
    children dancing *30*
    Christmas 190
    classes 91
    cookery lessons 129
    cost 35
    dentist visits 207
    discipline 206
    early twentieth century *37*
    Empire Day *206*
    entertainment 37
    holidays 40, 43
    hometime noise 207
    illness and death 41-3
    ink pens 206
    journey to school 180
    late 1800s *35*
    leaving age 92, 129
    lighting and heating 128, 205
    log book pages January 1891 *38-9*
    meals 31, 128
    milk distribution 161-2
    nit inspections 161
    patriotism 207
    plays 25
    police visit *46*
    pound day 207
    pulling the bell 204
    punishment book 206
    pupils 23, *35*, 40, 41, 44, 45, 46, 88-**9**, *89*
    schoolboy pranks 165-6, 207
    sports 61, *117*, *135*, 205, 208
    teachers 10, 31-2, 68, 88-9, 91, 161, 164, **205**, 210

218

tree-planting 2, 207-8
unauthorised smoking 164-5
visits by governors 166
welfare handouts 161
see also children
Braishfield Seven 21, 32, *110*, *111*, **132**, *133*, 134, **197-8**, *201*
Bramble Cottage 1
brick kilns 1, *58*, 92-3
Broom Hill Cottage **175**
Broomhill viii, 109
Brownies *see* Braishfield Brownies
Bryndlewood 70
buildings **175-8**
    see also named buildings
    eg. Orchard Cottage
Bull Grove Copse 2
Butcher's Farm *174*
Butterfield, William ix, 33, 34, 175
butterflies 155

Canister Cottage (Pucknall) *13*
Casbrook Common viii, 68, 160
chalk pits 213
Chalkpit Cottages **4**, 162
Chapel 1, 3, 30, 61, 63, 131
    Sunday School 94, 180
    see also Congregational Church;
    United Reformed Church
charity fundraising 32, 132
Cherry Hill 47, 48-9
Cherville Street 94
children *50*, *128*
    games played by 25, 205, 208, 213-14
    gangs 213
    given biscuits as treat 134
    given Coronation presents 134
    golliwog toy 89-90
    helping on farms 37, 40-1
    Infant Welfare Clinic 7
    nut gathering 40

in Paynes Hay Lane *71*
on recreation ground *126*, *165*
spud-bashing 55
toys 89-90
see also Braishfield School
Christian Aid 32
Christmas festivities 64, 89, 91, 109, 170, 179-80, 188-90, *202*, 208-9
Church Lane *20*, 30, 155
Church Room (Parish Room) 209
Church View 47
The Close 30, 155, *167*
    see also The Vicarage
Colsons Barn 155
Colsons Farm 3
Common Hill 63, 125, 133, 134, 151
Congregational Church *5*, 32, *131*, *177*
    see also Chapel; United Reformed Church
The Cottage 4, 155
council houses 125
country fair 21, 96-103, *97*, *98*, *102*
Cricket Club *see* Braishfield Cricket Club
Cromwell Cottage 17
Crook Bridge *1*
Crook Cottages 91
Crook Hill 1-5, 92, 137
Crook Hill Farm 52, 136, 162
Crouay 26-7, 101
Cubs *see* Braishfield Cubs

dairies and dairymen 72-4, 76, 80-1, 162
    see also farms and farming
Daisyfield 31
Dark Lane 4
dentists 207
doctors 7, 42, 211
Dog and Crook 20-1, 56, 69, 93-4, *93*, *104*, *106*, 125, 162, *168*, 169, 181, 192, *193*

219

fire 94, 104-6
domestic work 90, 92, 210
Dores Lane 115, 162
drink *see* food and drink
Dummers House 1, *6*, 17

education 31-2
   see also Braishfield School
Eldon Lane 72
Elm Grove Farm viii, *24*, 52-3, *57*, *58*, 78, **79**, *80*, **81**, 107, 133, 134, 166, *176*, 210
Elm Grove Farm Cottage *82*
entertainment
   American GIs 126
   beetle drives 131-2
   children's games 131-2
   concerts 20
   Coronation 133-4
   dances 69, 130-1, 187
   George Formby records 163
   magic lantern 37
   Morris dancing 21
   music 132
   scruff dog racing 99
   whist drives 131, 135
   see also Braishfield Music and Drama Society (BMADS); Braishfield Seven; Christmas; Women's Institute (WI), drama group
events
   Braishfield Seven Fete *201*
   Christmas Nativity play *202*
   Coronation Day *133-4*, *200*
   Empire Day *206*, 207
   fancy dress party *91*
   Jubilee Day *199*
   Millennium party 47
   Millennium village picnic and concert *203*
   Newport vs The Club Boxing Day football *199*
   opening of Village Hall *200*
   ordination celebration at Hereford *203*
   organist retirement party *200*
   Over Sixties Club outing *201*
   pageant marking centenary of church *167*
   Social Club fancy dress competition *86*
   tug-of-war at flower show *202*
Ex-Servicemen's Club 12
   see also Social Club

Fairbourne Cottages, family group *36*
Fairbourne Place **177**, *212*
Fairbourne Woods 17
Fairbournes Farm viii, *52*, **53**, *58*, *59*, 87, 88, *91*, **104**, *105*, 136, *161*, *169*, **177**, **178**
Farley Farm 107
Farley Lane 157
Farley Rectory 30, 189
farms and farming 32-3, 37, 40, 72, 88, 106-7, 166, 181, 210, 213
   changing patterns 51-2
   children helping 37, 40-1
   corn ricks *55*
   corn threshing *54*
   daffodils 52, 74-7
   ducks and pig sties *161*
   effect of weather 32
   harvest 32, 33, 40-1, 80, 88, 213
   horse and cart *24*
   horse-drawn binder *57*
   labourers 35
   link with pubs 55-6
   loading sheaves for threshing onto trailer *60*
   milking 72-4, *105*, 107, 148-50, 162, 210
   newly-made wagon *192*
   ownership 52-4
   ploughing *72*
   potato picking 133

steam-driven stationary baler *99*
stock movement 51
sugar beet 52
temporary work 182-3
threshing straw for thatching *172*
tractor and binder *52, 59*
tractor with seed drill *77*
unloading hay bales *104*
war years 54-5
widgeon thatching wheat *54*
see also animals and birds
Fernhill viii, 2, 157-9
Fernhill Farm 54, 109
fetes 40, 134, 187-8, *215*
First World War 17, 63, 134, 168
    Armistice 27, 185, 190
    farming 51-2
    handkerchief *90*
    life and death 185
    soldier *88*
fish and chip shop 87
flower shows *10,* 11, 94, 109, 134, *189*
food and drink 23, 24, 25, 31, 33, 54, 63, 70, 80, 81, 88, 91, 93, 96, 126, 134, 160, 161-2, 170, 179-80, 210-11
Football Club *see* Braishfield Football Club
Friendly Society Fete 188
fuel *see* heating and lighting

The Gardens 62-3, 127
ghosts 8, 15
Girl Guides *see* Braishfield Girl Guides
Greenacres 72
Guinness Race 195-**6**
Guy Fawkes celebrations 1, 47, 164
gypsies *see* Romanies

Hall Farm 2, 5, 16, 79
Hall Place Cottage *72*
Hall Place farm viii, *51, 52,* 72, 178
Hambledon Hunt 154

health
    illness and death 41-3
    spiders and woodworm 76-7
heating and lighting 205
    acetylene gas 121
    anthracite boiler 121-2
    candles 9, 180
    coal 3, 69, 91, 128, 180, 181
    electricity 9-10, 78, 125, 205
    oil 9, 69, 177, 180
    paraffin 87, 180
Highfield 72
Hill View 11, 31, 130, *165,* 189, *211*
Hilliers Nurseries 92, 186-7
holidays *128,* 208, 213
The Homestead 54, 93
horses *24, 52,* 54, *82,* 120, *122,* 164, 182, 185, 194
    at Romsey Show *81*
    burial 4
    carthorses *213*
    cob 82
    death of Ginger 211
    event 154-5
    gymkhanas 170
    hackney ponies 9, 79, 154
    Harveston Wattie 79
    hunting *22,* 153-4
    racehorses 154
    shire 80
    stables 3
    see also animals and birds
hospitals 7
hurdle enclosure *16*
hurdles and spars 2
Hursley 188
Hursley Estate 7, 75, *192,* 193
Hursley Hambledon Hunt 96
Hursley Hunt 4, 21, *22,* 109, *124,* **153-6***, 156*
    Boxing Day Meet *153*
Hursley Hunt Kennels 1, 162

Infant Welfare Clinic 7
inter-war years 9-12

Jermyns Lane 92
Jermyn's Wood 89

Kiln Lane 131
Kings Somborne 67, 72

laundry *see* washing and laundry
Laurel Cottage 192, *194*
The Lichens 61
lighting *see* heating and lighting
The Lodge 4, 7, 9, *11*, 29, 79, 169, 188, 190
Lower Braishfield *15*
Lower Slackstead *75*, 88
Lower Street 192

mains drainage 21
Malthouse Farm 23, *24*, 79
Malthouse Farm Cottage 76
The Manor 4, 6, 29, 62, 64, 79, 89, 91, 166, 188, 193, 208-9
  cross-roads *67*
  enlarging 29
  garden scenes *120*, *121*
  war years 120-3
  see also Pitt House
Megana Way 20
Merrie Meade Farm 49
Mesolithic site **109**
Michelmersh viii, 7, 181, 188
Michelmersh Church 16
Michelmersh Silver Band 94, 109
monks 21
Mothers' Union *112*

Necton Cottage 62
Ned's Corner 2
Newport House *59*
Newport Inn 20, 49, *51*, 54, 55, *56*, 69, **76**-7, *147*, *156*, **162**, 187

Newport Inn Farm 54, 55-6
Newport Lane 1, 3, 61, 63, 95, 152, 162, 163
  see also The Terrace
Newport Lane/Kiln Lane cottages *13*

The Old Forge 62, 65
Orchard Cottage 3, 4, **176**, *215*
Orchard Rise 3
Oxo cubes 213-14

Parish Room *see* Church Room
Parnholt Wood 81, 183, 184
Paynes Hay Farm viii, 9, 52, 53, *66*, 79, *182*
Paynes Hay Lane 62, 65, 70, *71*
pensioners' outing *201*
Pitt Farm viii, 79, 81
  family group *83*
Pitt Farm cottages *63*
Pitt House 4, *5*
  see also The Manor
police *46*, 98, 109, 169
Pond Cottages *30*, 53, 215, *216*
post office 3, 11-12, 63, *64*, 88, 95, 107, 130, 181
postmen 72, 136
pubs 1, 30, 32, 49
  see also Dog and Crook; Newport Inn; Wheatsheaf Inn
Pucknall 134, 189
Pucknall Farm 2, 21, *60*, 75, 115
Pucknall House 6

railways 185-6, 211
recreation ground 12, *126*, 130, 164, *165*, 173, *207*
The Rectory 30-1, 32, 213
Red Cross group *130*
Roman Field 55
Roman remains viii, **57-9**
Romanies (gypsies) 67

222

Romsey 12, 25, 31, 70, 80, 92, 95, 129, 193
Romsey Cadets *129*
Romsey Hospital 94
Romsey Over Sixties Club outing *201*
Rose Cottage 47, *48*, *50*
Roxana 151
Royal Garrison Artillery 17, 185
Rupert Cottage 61

Sauce Hill 68
Scorey's Hill 181
Second World War 48, 190
    American GIs 56, 126, 130, 161
    anti-aircraft guns 126
    ATS lady *9*
    Battle of Britain 68
    bomb damage 80, 127
    D-Day 124, 126
    deliveries 69
    engineering work 92
    entertainment 69, 130
    evacuees/evacuation 23-5, *23*, 127-8, **209**-10
    farming 52, 54-5
    gas masks 69
    German aeroplane 25
    GI wedding group *85*
    Home Guard 68-9, 79, 123-4, *123*, 186
    landgirls 25, 69, *84*, **148**-50
    Local Defence Volunteers 123
    post-war black market 162
    POWs 104, 162, 170
    railways 186
    rationing 24, 56
    searchlights 160
    victory celebrations 160-1
    village life 120-4
    work exemptions 65
Secondary School 31-2
servants 29, 190

sexton 3
The Shanty **176**
    see also Worsley Lodge
Sharpes Farm viii, *150*
shooting parties **136**
shops and shopping 11, 16, 20, 30, 63, 81, *94*, 95, 129-30, **151-2**, 184
    advertising remains 151-2, 164
    boots and shoes 3
    buying cigarettes 164
    change of use 71
    closing down 107, 130
    fishmongers 107
    General Stores 107
    greengrocers 20
    grocers 2, 69
    hard life 107-8
    Home and Colonial stores 107
    ice cream tricycle 70
    International Stores 107
    Lights Tobacconist and Confectionery 92
    Newport Lane 152
    Old Village Stores 163-**4**, **210**-11
    opposite the school 151-2
    Pearce's Bakery 20
    Second World War 69, 70
    sweet shops 95
Slackstead 2, 189
Social Club 12, 30, *86*, 135, *199*, *201*, *202*
    Boxing Day football match *201*
    see also Ex-Servicemen's Club
South View *2*, 63, *64*
Southampton 7, 12, 68, 122
Spanish seamen 162-3
Spinney Corner 30
sports
    cricket 2, 32, **144-6**, 164, 180, 213-14
    darts 94, *107*, *147*
    football 27, 32, *61*, **138-43**, *199*

223

go-karting 137
netball teams *117, 135, 204*
PT *165, 207*
school *61, 117, 135*, 205, 208
stoolball 25, 205
see also Braishfield Cricket Club; Braishfield Football Club
The Square **3**, 16, 47-50, 63, 92, 107
Standon 74-5
Sunday Schools 212
   group photo *131*
   picnic group *95*
   treats and outings 40, 94, 131-2, 180-1
Sunshine Home for Blind Babies 132
Swallowfield 63

Taunton Vale 82
telephones 10, 129, 162
television filming 98, 115-19
Temperance Band of Hope *see* Band of Hope
The Terrace 63, 163, **178**
   see also Newport Lane
Test Valley Archaeology Committee (TVAC) 157
thatch
   pub roof burnt 94, 105-6
   threshing straw *172*
   wet sack on roof 93-4
   wheat field *54*
Thelwell, Norman **47-50**
Timsbury 88
trades and tradesmen 162
   agricultural engineers 192
   artesian well-boring 92
   bakers 2, 7, 11, 20, 63, 69, 81, 95, 129, 167, 181, 193, 210-11
   barbers/hairdressers 67, 162, 163
   blacksmiths 3, 62, 65-8, 93, 122, 154, 167
   brickmaking 181, 193
   builders *63*, 162
   butchers 20, 69, *69*, 92, 107, 166, 193
   carpenters 61-2, *63*, 162, 181
   carriers 181-2
   carters 80
   chimney sweeps 162
   coal merchant *181*
   cooks 49, 88
   engineering workshop 61
   gardeners *30*, 134-5, 185, 186-7
   gravediggers 3
   hoopmakers 16-19, *17, 18*, 179, 183-5
   lengthmen (road men) 51, 127, 163
   milkmen 69
   plumbing 125
   ratcatcher *172*
   shoe and boot repairers 3
   spinning *101*
   timber carter 3
   tree-felling **183**-4
   undertakers 162, 181
   wheelwrights 162, 192
transport 20, 67-8, 95, 109, 120, 129, 162, 167, 193
   bicycles 67, 68, 70, 90, 104, *127*, 162, 182, 193, *195*, 208
   buses 12, 20, 95, 109, 208
   butcher's van *69*
   coach trip to Weymouth *85*
   grocer's van 164
   motor cars 49, 62, 67-8, 78, 81, *121*, 130, **208**
   motorcycles *137*, 162, *216*
   petrol rationing 6
   sugar beet train 52
   taxis 6, 63
   traction/steam engines *86*, 96, 98-**9**, **100**, *171*, **171**, *173*
   Trojan diesel van 167
Trinity Monday Fair 31

United Reformed Church ix, *131*
   Bible presentation to Junior Church *113*
   Christmas Nativity play *202*
   see also Chapel; Congregational Church

vergers 187
The Vicarage 30, 167
   see also The Close
Vickers Armstrong 92, 123
Village Band 3, 12, 134
   see also Braishfield Brass Band
village characters 174
   aeroplane constructor/agricultural machine operator 171-3
   artesian well-borer *92*
   battery and bulb seller 163
   blacksmith 167
   dairyman 162
   farmer 166
   gardeners *30*, 121, 167-8
   grumbling man 127
   haircutter 163
   hoopmaker *17*
   lady of the Manor 166
   man with two thumbs 162
   man who feared snakes 170
   motherly woman 169-70
   motorcycle daredevil 170-1
   organ pipe blower *30*
   pub landlord 168-9
   road maintenance man 163
   shopkeeper *184*
Village Hall 26, 70, 101
   opening party *200*
   sponsored bicycle ride *195*

walking 25, 36-7, 65, 193, 195-6, 208
War Memorial 3, *11*, 12, *61*, 63, 76, 88, 129, 181, 190, 195
washing and laundry 7, 88, 125-6

water 87, 92-3, 125, 192, 211-12
   brought to village 9
   pumps *211*
   shortages 7
weather 32, 35, 36-7
   Aurora Borealis 88
   war years 123
weather vanes 79
wells 92-3, *92*, 125, 181, 211-12
Wheatsheaf Inn 1, 2, 20, 27, 69, 134, 151, *156*, 162, *163*, 180
Willett's Farm 66
Winchester viii, 6, 21, 30, 90, 98, 182
windmill 4
Windmill Cottage 9
Women's Institute (WI) 10, 69
   dances 30, 32, 130-1
   drama group *12*
   Dutch Day garden party *110*
   fete *215*
   group outside Hall *7*
   Hall *14*
   Hut 7, 20, 32, 130-1
Women's Land Army 55, 148-50
Woodley Village Hall 130
Woodman's Cottage (Farley) 2
Woolley Green *75*, 190
Woolley Green House *15*
Woolley House 2
Worsley Lodge 129, 151, *176*
   see also The Shanty
Worzel Gummidge **115-19**

Yew Tree Cottage **30**
Young Farmers' Club Rally, Broadlands *65*
youth club 130, 131

Photographs and other images

Courtesy of Winchester Museums Service are the photographs of All Saints' Church. (Boothman) *PWCM 4364*, All Saints' Church (Buildings) *PWCM4366* and Lower Braishfield (Vanished Buildings) *PWCM 4304*.

Courtesy of Hampshire Record Office are the photographs of All Saints' Church clock tower (Boothman) *147M87/1/345*, Braishfield School log books (Chant) and Broomhill Cottage (Buildings) *65M89/73/2*.

Courtesy of the Hampshire Chronicle are the photographs of hounds leaving kennels (Bartlam) *3883*, the Village Hall opening party (Events) *349/96*, Albert Cobbold receiving shield (Foxcroft) *176/127*, Braishfield School winning netball team (Marshall) *336/88*, hounds passing Braishfield House. (Rawson-Smith) *205/107*, Braishfield Seven last show in the WI Hall (Stewart) *344/77* and Braishfield schoolchildren with Police Commissioner (Schools) *334/87*.

Courtesy of BFI Stills and the copyright of Tony Nutley photographer are the two photographs of Worzel Gummidge (Marshall) *327862 and 327863*.

Courtesy of the Southern Daily Echo is the photograph of Margaret Stewart spinning at Braishfield Country Fair (Hughes).

Courtesy of Hampshire Magazine are the two photographs of Mr Scorey hoopmaking and hoopmaking tools (Baird).

Courtesy of The Antiquaries Journal is the photograph of a beaker at Broom Hill (McCall).

Courtesy of Canon Samuel Boothman and the copyright of Norman Thelwell, the artist, is the woodcut for 'Crookhill to Farley Mount' (Boothman).

The photographs of felling an oak tree by hand (Scorey), Joan Parsons bathing beauty (Stewart) and Newport Inn Darts Team (Teams) are the copyright of photographer Terry Viney.

The photograph of Norma and Rhona Thelwell (Chant) is the copyright of Woman and Home Magazine.

The map of Braishfield 2003 was created by Sophie Allen.

Donors

Donations from village organisations, businesses and individuals were crucial to get the project off the ground and those who have generously supported us are listed below.

Mr and Mrs G Bennett
The Boothman family
Professor and Mrs D Brown
Braishfield Horticultural Society
Braishfield Manor Cross Country Course
Braishfield Music and Drama Society
Braishfield Parish Council
Braishfield Parochial Church Council
Braishfield School Association
Braishfield Social Club
Braishfield United Reformed Church
Braishfield Village Association
Braishfield Women's Institute
R D Brazier
A H Cheater (Funeral Directors)
Close Management Services Limited
J M Cook
George Gale and Company Limited
Mr and Mrs R Groves
J N Landscapes Limited
Dr and Mrs P Quarendon
Mr and Mrs R Smith
Smith Bradbeer and Company Limited
Test Valley Travel Limited
Mr and Mrs P White

Grant

We could not have published this book of memories to the standard and quality to which we aspired without the financial support of the Local Heritage Initiative. We were fortunate to have the encouragement of Kevin Haugh and Lisa Birch. LHI is a partnership between the Heritage Lottery Fund, Nationwide Building Society and the Countryside Agency.

Local Heritage *initiative*